Inch By Inch
It's A Cinch

Inch By Inch
It's A Cinch

How to Succeed At Anything—
One Small Step At A Time

Dr. Gary S. Goodman

Published 2018 by Gildan Media LLC
aka G&D Media
www.GandDmedia.com

FIRST EDITION 2018

Front Cover design by David Rheinhardt of Pyrographx

Interior design by Meghan Day Healey of Story Horse, LLC

Library of Congress Cataloging-in-Publication Data is available upon request

ISBN: 978-1-7225-0010-8

10   9   8   7   6   5   4   3   2   1

Contents

Introduction and Overview

G_o to NASA's website and click on the pictures the Hubble telescope has taken. You'll see amazing nebulas, cradles of new stars, blazing colors, and infinite details.

We think there are 100 billion stars in a typical galaxy, and there are at least 100 billion galaxies in the known universe.

This thought can be overwhelming.

Complexity of any type can make your jaw drop and your heart stop, and cause instant brain freeze. In other words, if we think something is too complicated, we shut down mentally and emotionally.

We can only handle a certain number of inputs at once. Given our limited bandwidth, if we receive too many signals, we overload.

This explains why most people don't get much done, or certainly not enough to have the kind of life they want to lead.

They see a result, such as a neighbor with a flashy new car, or a person with a great job at Google, or some other desirable achievement, and believe it is way beyond their modest skill to accomplish.

The good news is we are like those celestial bodies, stars, and planets, and we comply with the same laws. One of them is Newton's famous First Law of Motion, which states a body in motion tends to stay in motion and a body at rest tends to stay at rest.

Once we get under way, we have momentum, and it is relatively easy to keep going.

I keep myself entertained on long drives by periodically watching my fuel-consumption monitor. At first, in traffic before I reach the open highway, I'll get lousy mileage. But then, after ten or more freeway miles, I put on the cruise control and I practically double my mileage right away.

The gas gauge tells an important story. My car consumes a lot of energy at the beginning of a trek, but it takes less fuel to keep going. And over the course of many hours, the fuel economy is optimized.

Einstein said that *a mark of genius is the ability to reduce the complex to the simple.*

If so, then I may be a genius (and you can become one too), because my profession consists of making order out of chaos, helping people of all kinds to get more out of their careers and businesses and lives.

And I do it mainly through simplifying and redirecting focus.

I'm a consultant, a coach, and a teacher. I identify the next step folks need to take to get from A to B. Put these micro-moves into a sequence, and you have a plan.

Test the plan to see if it works. When it does, you'll have a routine that you can use to create and grow enduring success.

Whenever you feel stuck, or you're in what one writer called a "gumption trap," where you're making little or no progress and you're stagnating, you have a very basic problem.

You don't know what to do next.

You are so overwhelmed by infinite options, none of which seem promising, that choosing one seems no better than choosing another.

Or, more to my point, you don't know how much to do *initially*.

So typically, you don't choose, and you stay where you are. Or worse, you regress, going backward to a more primitive level of being and doing.

It happens too often to too many of us. But there's a way to break through and find our way back to achievement.

Do you remember how we learned the alphabet? It was one letter and one sound at a time.

How do we eat? We eat one bite at a time.

This is so elementary that you might be thinking that it is beneath you, and you're way beyond what I'm saying.

But if you ever get stuck, find yourself in a rut, or feel depressed or disempowered, believe me, you've forgotten this principle.

You are then probably asking, "Why me?" instead of "What's next?"

Recently I wrote a book and recorded an audiobook titled *Selling Is So Easy, It's Hard*.

If you ask a slumping seller why he or she isn't producing, you're likely to hear a variety of excuses. Their sales lists are outdated, their products too expensive, nobody wants to talk to them.

But the real culprit is they have stopped doing the simple things, the blocking and tackling of sales. They're making fewer contacts, resulting in fewer buying decisions, resulting in diminished sales.

"Yes, I guess I need to make more contacts," they might acknowledge, but this truth is also deceiving.

In the *big picture*, or Hubble-photograph perspective, this is what they need to do. Theoretically, they need to make a huge number of contacts, because we know that most prospects will reject their offers.

However, the tiny truth is they need to make the NEXT CONTACT.

For now, just one contact will do.

It will get the ball rolling, dusting off the cobwebs, while generating positive momentum toward the overall goal.

Motivational speakers urge us to have bigger goals, but they make a mistake. They don't emphasize nearly enough taking baby steps to reach those goals.

That's what we're doing here to succeed, because inch by inch, anything is a cinch. We see this in all walks of life.

Ted Williams, the Hall of Fame outfielder for the Boston Red Sox, and the last person to hit over .400 in a season, offered this sage advice:

"Get a good pitch to hit!"

When I was playing Pony League baseball, I heard a version of this. I was in the deepest slump ever of my nascent baseball career.

Empathizing with me, feeling the pain of every strikeout, my dad took to chanting little mantras from the bleachers.

The one that stands out most in my memory is:

"It just takes one, Gary!"

Parental tips, barked from on high, usually have little influence. I'm not sure this suggestion empowered me to hit more often, to hit more forcefully, or to end my slumps.

But as social scientists would say, the wisdom in this suggestion had a mighty "sleeper effect" on me.

I have taken the "It just takes one" philosophy to heart many times in my career and life, and I'm always finding effectiveness and new kernels of truth in it.

I'm going to share them with you in this program. With this concept alone, you can be exponentially more powerful and successful in your career and your life.

I am the best-selling author of about twenty books and a dozen audio programs. One of my titles is *The Law of Large Numbers: How to Make Success Inevitable*.

In that program I say that if you do enough of practically anything, you'll become good at it. Do more than that, and success will be yours. Exceed even that successful level of activity, and you'll become a legend.

The concept is clear, and it works—marvelously. But the problem most people have is with beginning.

They find it easy to continue wheeling along once the wheel has been manufactured.

What is more difficult is overcoming inertia and getting under way. We need to take baby steps, and inch our way off the starting line.

That's what we're focusing on here. You've heard the saying, "Well begun is half done." There's great truth in this.

I've observed something about those that achieve great things, career success, and ultimate fulfillment.

They are great "starters." They do something, taking that proverbial first step, which Confucius said initiates a journey of a thousand leagues.

In spite of what some may think, most of us are very good finishers. Especially when we've had initial success with the first step, putting one foot ahead of the next feels easy and completely natural.

I've reduced the whole process of starting to an essential insight: it just takes one, you-name-it-fill-in-the-blank, to succeed right now and over the course of your life.

This notion's applications are practically limitless.

Appreciating it can break you out of slumps, end your procrastination habit, build sales, and raise incomes. It can be your watchphrase as you navigate life in search of suitable mates and best friends.

It will help you to put a very different spin on rejection and failure. And crucially, it will bring everything down to a manageable perspective.

I do a lot of career coaching, helping people to create novel jobs for themselves while showing them how to get paid far more than they're worth.

I feel a special kinship with salespeople, because I have had my own consulting practice for years. This means I have sold hundreds of engagements, all of which required selling skills.

Though you may doubt this at first, I've found it takes just one successful script to make a salesperson, or even a business, succeed.

Let me give you a personal example. This is how I started a super-successful consulting practice.

I developed a new seminar for businesses based on my occupational experience in sales and management, augmented by a specialized knowledge of communications that I had gleaned from eight years of study. I sought to popularize my course by getting universities to market it.

But first, I had to sell them on selling me!

Universities are not fleet of foot. As a rule, they change slowly, and they don't adopt and endorse the "new" without some heavy persuasion and deep thought.

At least that is their reputation.

I had to dismiss all of these apparent limitations because I needed their help, and I needed it ASAP.

How could I persuade them to offer my course in the next ninety to a hundred and twenty days? That was when my money would run out from regular college teaching, which I had decided to leave.

I needed a script, but not a robotic or high-pressure document that would make them recoil in disgust.

I needed a stealth script, one that did its persuasive magic without being detected.

But I realized something, without thinking it completely through.

If I succeeded with JUST ONE UNIVERSITY, getting them to offer my one-day course, and then, if that one class succeeded, there would be no limit to the number of schools I could partner with.

I just needed a prototype, a beta test site, just one initial institutional partner. To snare that one supporter, I needed just one short, persuasive conversational path.

So I wrote one, and in the process I discovered what I call "perfect questions."

A perfect question is so well-constructed that it gets the listener to think these three things: (1) I have a need; (2) that need is important; and (3) I want Gary's help to satisfy it.

I called a nearby campus that offered courses to businesspeople. After introducing myself and mentioning I was a college professor, I said:

"I've developed a new class for businesses and I was wondering how we might pursue the prospect of offering it at your school."

That is one super-short, super-specific, and super-successful script.

Here's what the conservative deans and directors thought after hearing this perfect question: (1) We do need to attract more businesses to campus; (2); business enrollees are an important source of revenue for us; and (3) Gary seems to have just the right credentials to team up with.

California State University, Los Angeles was my first partner. Within eighteen months, thirty-five universities were sponsoring that seminar of mine. It became a smash hit. Students loved it; so did the universities, which did very well with the enrollment income.

And I launched a very successful training and consulting practice that would sustain me for decades.

From that ONE seminar and ONE script, I multiplied my income by more than ten times over eighteen months.

I did one of my trainings at a relatively small campus, and the huge business publisher Prentice-Hall noticed. A senior editor contacted me and asked, "Do you want to write a book?"

"I'll do better than that," I replied. "I'll write two."

Actually, I wrote six books in five years for Prentice-Hall, and three or more of them became best sellers.

Again, all of this came from just ONE seminar, ONE school, and ONE script.

I combined the power of one with the Law of Large Numbers and succeeded wildly, becoming independent, doing what I loved and still love: teaching and sharing knowledge.

Do you know what prevents most folks from getting into shape, shedding pounds, and firming their forms? The answer is so simple that it will seem utterly trivial.

The ONE obstacle is doing just ONE thing toward that goal.

I have a set of weights beneath my desk.

If I can get myself to simply pick up one of them and to do ONE movement, the next movement will follow automatically.

Then the next day, I just need to do that one repetition to spawn several.

Take that first walk down the block. You don't need fancy athletic shoes or a note from your doctor.

You need to open the door ONCE and take that first step.

You may have heard that we should drink something like twelve glasses of water every day to promote a healthy constitution.

If you think of twelve, you probably won't do it. The idea of twelve full glasses of liquid sounds as if it would drown us.

Twelve are too many to contemplate. Even one full glass may be over the top for you. Fair enough: go to your water source and pour in one mouthful and drink that. Refill until full, and then return later to do the same.

A quota of twelve glasses is reached with one sip at a time, as Confucius might have said.

We're all beset by doubts from time to time. Instead of eagerly jumping into the game, we stand safely on the sidelines.

When challenged, we retreat. Our *chi*, or life's essence, seems to jump under the bed and hide. We've gone from being at-cause to being at-effect, from active to reactive.

I've found that when the blues set in, I just need ONE piece of good news.

Mark Twain said something similar when he quipped, "I can live for three months on a good compliment!"

So go get one.

Manufacture a piece of good news. Starting with one person, go on to surround yourself with folks that sincerely find you to be good company.

I did this the other day at the park. Waiting for my kids to finish their tennis class, I spotted another parent, so I plunked myself down on the grass.

He seemed disheartened, so I decided to snap him out of it by making dumb jokes. After one tickler in particular, he cracked up. As I was leaving with the kids, he said, "Thanks for the company!"

Want to be cheered up? Cheer up just one other person.

Works every time.

I believe that looking to do just one thing, taking a small step in the direction of our dreams, is exceedingly powerful. Here's a comment about the power of starting that's often attributed to the great German poet and philosopher Goethe:

> *Until one is committed, there is hesitancy, the chance to draw back—concerning all acts of initiative (and creation), there is one elementary truth that ignorance of which kills countless ideas and splendid plans: That the moment one definitely commits oneself, then Providence moves too. All sorts of things occur to help one that would never otherwise have occurred. A whole stream of events issues from the decision, raising in one's favor all manner of unforeseen incidents and meetings and material*

assistance, which no man could have dreamed would have come his way.

Whatever you can do, or dream you can do, begin it. Boldness has genius, power, and magic in it. Begin it now.

This is a grand quote, redolent with power and command. But don't let it daunt you.

When we hear that we need to "commit," it is easy to get confused. Commitment sounds HUGE, overwhelming, and earthshaking.

To me, committing is anything but; it is simple and straightforward. It amounts to doing JUST ONE THING in furtherance of your wishes. Repetition comes later, usually after we've noticed we're under way and we've garnered some initial success.

Thinking that things must be complex is the norm, and it is self-defeating. It leads to perfectionism.

Perfectionists tend to accomplish very little in life, and they aren't very happy as a whole. They believe that every wrinkle must be ironed out before dressing. The winds have to be just right to go sailing, and the tides perfect to kayak.

The way things are, the current level of your training and preparedness, are never complete enough or quite right for the perfectionist. And thus perfectionists stall. They get stuck and stay stuck.

The people that accomplish the most in life have a different philosophy, more akin to: Ready! FIRE! Aim!

An accomplished executive at Xerox put it this way when agreeing to take action on something I suggested: "Around here, it is far easier to ask for forgiveness than for permission."

In the same vein, you may have heard there are three types of people: (1) those that make things happen; (2) those that watch things happen; and (3) those that scratch their heads and ask, "What happened?"

You want to be the first type, to be the person that makes things happen. This requires starting, taking the first step, trying something.

Robert M. Pirsig wrote a very good novel titled *Zen and the Art of Motorcycle Maintenance.* His main character is an English professor in Bozeman, Montana. Trying for the umpteenth time to make it easier for his students to write their papers, he broke the process down to its elements.

They were asked to write about the city of Bozeman. One girl lamented that the topic was too big and complex and she didn't know where to begin.

"OK, start by describing a single street," Pirsig suggested.

"No, still too much to cover," she countered.

"Start with one house."

This, too, was overwhelming.

Finally he persuaded her to write about one brick in one house on one street in Bozeman, Montana.

That she could do.

We need to find that one brick as well, and start there.

In *City Slickers,* a fine film comedy from yesteryear, cowboy Jack Palance and city slicker Billy Crystal exchange notes about this idea, except they're on horseback somewhere in what looks like the old West.

Raising one index finger, Palance asks, "Do you know what the secret of life is?"

"Your finger?" wisecracks Crystal.

"One thing. Just one thing," Palance answers. "You stick to that and everything else don't mean (expletive)."

"That's great, but what's the one thing?" Crystal asks.

"That's what you gotta figure out."

Exactly. That's what we need to determine in all of the significant areas of life. What is the one thing we need to focus on at this time that can make all the difference?

I mentioned that I'm a teacher. This is a catchall term for the fact that I train people in business and coach them individually and I'm also an instructor at universities.

It has always bothered me when I'm teaching and my students are distracted.

They may be texting on their phones, or whispering to each other.

Here I am, putting myself out to transfer important information, which I may have never before articulated in a certain way, and some folks are going to miss it entirely.

It's a waste.

I was delivering a major convention speech in Las Vegas, and the distractions were everywhere. People were streaming in and out, chips in their hands, their minds on winning and losing.

But I knew to ignore them, to select from the crowd one of the many who was genuinely listening and to "dedicate" my talk to him or her.

Likewise, there is almost always someone in an audience that is unreachable. Work as I might to ferret out their questions and to determine what information they need to know, they just don't receive what I'm sending.

On speaker and teaching evaluations, though they are anonymous, that one person often gives the lowest score of the bunch.

Now get this. Every other score can be off the charts, super-high, but what is my tendency? It is to dwell on the one that got away, the person I didn't reach.

And I've found there isn't enough information in that negative score or downbeat comment for me to help me remedy anything.

My talks are serious, but I add a lot of improvisational humor to them. Just last week, one of my seminar attendees said, "Thanks for making it so much fun."

For her, our two days together flew by, and for me as well.

But that disgruntled person, the one that downgraded me, might have muttered, "The humor was a little cheesy."

What does that mean? Which joke didn't you like? Should I make these sessions more serious? And if I do, will I lose the attention and appreciation of everyone else?

Some schools are smart about evaluations. They toss out the lowest individual score, averaging the remainder to determine the overall level of student satisfaction.

Still, I receive the raw score sheets, including the one that is officially excluded. Once I've seen it, it is hard to blot it out of my consciousness.

But that is the ONE THING I have to do.

"You can't win them all" and "You can't please all of the people all of the time" are phrases designed to help us to avoid overweighing anomalies—individual circumstances that are not the norm.

Which leads us to this insight: Sometimes we need to find or to discover the one EXCEPTION to a rule that will get us to where we need to go.

I usually rely on publishers to distribute my books and audios. They are in the business of marketing knowledge products, and they're good at it.

In selling some of these projects, I have broken a famous rule of engagement with many of these publishers. I'll purposely phone them to inquire about their interest in a title instead of emailing.

I get the fact that most of these folks are readers, and books are read, so sending out a printed version of what I have in mind can be helpful, and I will get it over to them.

In time, that is.

But I need a faster turnaround than weeks to months to hear back about an idea.

In one case, I queried a publisher and didn't receive its response until a month before the book was to be published by a competing house. It took eight months simply to receive their acknowledgment letter.

So I call publishers instead, though they explicitly say, "No phone calls, please!" in their pronouncements about how they prefer to be contacted.

I'll leave a voice mail, short and to the point, but enticing and credible. And invariably, after I've contacted a dozen or so, I'll hear back from three to six of them who ask to see more from me about that project.

This "hit rate" or success rate is fairly astonishing. Plus, it is fast.

By using the ONE channel they do not want me to use, I distinguish myself from the zillions of other writers that are competing for their attention.

You may be wondering, how many publishers have actually said, "You're breaking the rule, Gary, and we refuse to consider a query by phone"?

ZERO—at least that I can recall. Perhaps they are among those that don't invite me to follow with a full proposal. But if I'd used email, there would have been a much higher proportion of those.

Frankly, rules are OK, because we know the adage: for every rule there is an exception.

I'll be happy to be that ONE exception. And you should be too.

My dad had an interesting view of rule breaking. For example, he wanted me to attend the college he graduated from, his alma mater.

I said, "Dad I don't want to go there, and anyway, I had to apply six months ago to even be considered."

"I'll make a call," he confidently replied.

Later that day or the next, beaming like a wizard, he announced, "You're in."

"I'm in what?"

"My school. I got you accepted. All you need to do is meet with the dean."

Shaking my head, I couldn't believe it.

Then he told me HIS rule, his one overriding belief in circumstances such as these.

"Gary, let me say this quite clearly. There's always room for ONE MORE."

This may not apply to riding in elevators, where too many bodies will stress the cables, but it is surprising how often this principle holds true.

Let me give you an even more improbable example of exception finding.

Most actors that come to Hollywood beat a familiar path. They try to find roles, any roles at first, to develop their credits, their résumés. They also try to find an agent that will represent them, to get them readings and auditions.

There's nothing wrong with this "rule"; everyone starts out this way.

But there are exceptions, and my dad decided to create one for me after he saw me act in various productions.

He decided to find me an agent.

How do most people go about it? They cold-call agencies directly, send over photos, and badger anyone that will speak to them for an appointment.

This doesn't end well for most applicants.

It is more likely that they'll get an agent by referral,

or one will spot them doing an obscure role in a production.

Realizing this, my father decided to manufacture a referral.

He called the major studios and got casting directors on the phone. His logic was simple.

They *hire* actors though agents, probably relying on one or two for most roles. Find out which agents casting directors like, and then call those agents.

Dad heard the same agent's name from a few sources. He called him and said:

"Casting directors at these studios highly recommended you to represent my son."

Honored by the compliments, after one agent heard about a few of my credits he consented to an interview with me, and voilà! He signed me up and sent me to auditions within a few weeks.

This telescoped what could have been years in the making had Dad not determined the smart small step that he could take to produce a giant leap toward the goal.

Most of us make a mistake when we set goals. We believe we have to map out all of the actions that it will take to reach them.

But these roadmaps are unknowable and never completely accurate when we make them sitting in our chairs.

As pioneering semanticist Alfred Korzybski said, "The map is not the territory."

We need to break out of mental abstractions and get into the concrete world of "facts on the ground," as they are called.

I just read one American astronaut's description of being sent to the moon. He spoke of NASA having "slung" the spacecraft in the general direction of the target. But every ten minutes, he went on to say, the crew had to steer the device, making adjustment after adjustment during the trip.

Ultimately, the moon ship arrived within yards of its intended goal.

Imagine you're taking a cross-country car trip at night. Your map will put you on the right road, but you'll never be able to see from where you are to the end of your journey.

Your headlights can help you to see only two hundred feet ahead. How can you get across three thousand miles of road while only being able to see the next two hundred feet?

The answer is found in the question. You ONLY need to see two hundred feet ahead to traverse the country!

Inch by inch, any journey or task or goal is a cinch. Yard by yard, it's hard.

Speaking of road trips, have you ever stopped in a traditional diner for a meal?

They're all different, but in one way they're almost completely the same.

Near the cash register, framed on the wall, you'll spot the first dollar that establishment ever earned.

A dollar won't buy anything on the menu, but the meaning of that buck is priceless.

That dollar is where it all began. That was the first

inch that became a business that went on to support countless lives.

Remember, it just takes ONE.

In the sections that follow, I'm going to give you specific pointers about applying this inch-by-inch thinking to achieving any goal.

You'll see how job hunting, starting businesses, finding a great mate, becoming wealthy, getting into great physical shape, and achieving happiness and a fulfilling life can all be achieved in easy-to-take baby steps.

Like a coach training a world-class runner, I can't wait to show you how to break the tape at the end of the race.

The best way to do that is to motivate you to enter the race and prepare you to burst out of the blocks.

Ready, set, here we go!

1

Anybody Can Conquer Procrastination

This book is all about taking action, even of the smallest kind, and this is exactly what procrastinators avoid doing.

So our first order of business in this chapter is to disable the procrastination habit.

My definition of procrastination is putting off until a later time something that should be done sooner, or right now.

By putting it off, you lose something. The cost could be financial. It could also be interpersonal—a relationship loss. Almost always, delaying exacts an emotional cost—in you.

You dislike yourself because you haven't met a challenge head-on. You've hidden under the covers when you should have boldly advanced on the world, in your pajamas if necessary.

Why do we procrastinate? One big reason is that we may be self-destructive. We get in our own way, stubbing our toes on purpose.

This comes from low self-esteem. We don't believe we're worthy, and to prove it we set ourselves up for failure.

Comedian Woody Allen quipped that "80 percent of success is showing up." If we're perennially late to engagements, late for the bus, late in paying our bills when we have enough dough to do it, we simply do not want success, do we?

Success must, on some level, be perceived as painful, and failure as pleasurable, correct?

Convoluted as this thinking seems, it is logical if we don't think much of ourselves and believe we do not deserve life's goodies.

I worked for a dynamic software company that was experiencing rapid growth. It went public, so it was flush with money. One afternoon I ran into the CEO as she was eating lunch out.

We ate together, and out of curiosity I asked her, "Did you always plan on the company becoming big, or did it just sort of happen?"

"Big!" she exclaimed, almost missing a swallow.

That didn't quite compute for me, because I had a different mindset. As Paul Hawken said in a nifty little book, *Growing a Business*, growth should be organically nurtured and should not be pushed.

That thought was my limitation, as I would see later on, when my consulting business could have grown to staggering proportions. But I was happy with what I had.

Now, I believe that the CEO's take was superior. If you can grow a business so that it is big and it gets there fast, what's wrong with that? That's certainly a typical image of succeeding in the marketplace, isn't it?

Today I do not attribute my relative lack of ambition to super-low self-esteem, but it was definitely lower than that of the driven CEO. I procrastinated in delegating many of my administrative and marketing functions to other people, and in doing so I missed the boat of growth.

Still, by most measures and by my internal standards at the time, I did very well.

Procrastination can be sneaky in this way. You may be getting a lot of things done, so how could anyone accuse you of putting things off? You should be spared the criticism, correct?

But in our heart of hearts, we know something is off.

Activity, though essential, isn't a 100 percent prescription for success. We need to be doing the *right* things, not doing just anything, or, as some folks call it, doing merely the get-by.

When we think of the worst procrastinators, people who are utterly frozen come to mind. They don't seem to do anything. They're stuck. They seem to be encased in ice.

Certainly this describes some of the worst sufferers, but we can conclusively say that, at any given time, all of us are procrastinating about something or other.

Complicating our understanding is the fact that occasionally procrastinating can be GOOD and BENE-FICIAL!

Some activities that we are avoiding simply shouldn't be done at all. They may require so much of our time that they prevent us from accomplishing other valuable things. Or our instincts may be warning us, beneath the threshold of awareness, that a particular path should not be taken. It could be the voice of caution, such as one I heard when I pulled out of a blind space in a parking lot.

A car suddenly swooshed by that would have clipped me had I shown less patience.

Which leads to this point: Procrastination may be patience, disguised. What seems like a vice could be a virtue.

If you aren't certain about the benefit in fully leaping into something, then taking a more measured approach is wise. Try moving forward in inches instead of feet and yards.

This is especially sage advice if you're dealing with sellers that are trying to hustle you into buying without sufficient consideration of the merits of the offer.

Con men and women, those that seek to fleece the innocent, are also called "hustlers," for a good reason. By creating artificial urgency, they hope to disarm the self-protective instinct to slow the process down.

Dragging your feet when you are being hustled is certainly no vice. And it summons to mind the conventional wisdom in "sleeping on" certain offers that come our way.

Successful corporate managers typically appreciate their less experienced staffers that bring them new ideas and potential opportunities to pursue. They listen diligently and dutifully. And then, quite purposely, they tuck those glittering ideas away for a while.

If the ideas "age well," and they still seem worthwhile days or weeks or months later, they are then aired and discussed, and action is taken.

So there are exceptions to the notion that procrastinating is 100 percent deleterious. It can be a valuable control on doing something that should be done later, or not at all.

What most folks want to conquer is destructive procrastination. This sort can spring from several sources.

1. **Let's not and say we did**. We may find so little pleasure in the process of accomplishing a task that we choose the pleasures of distraction instead. Relentlessly we check our email. Don't want to get your taxes done by April 15, or even by the end of the extension deadline, October 15? Of course—so do anything more pleasurable instead. Sometimes we even take on tasks that we hate, but just hate less. Washing the car comes to mind, because compared to doing taxes, that's a blast. And we can pat ourselves on the back for at least accomplishing something.

2. **I don't have a clue about how to do this.** We may have signed up for a class that requires advance training that we don't have. But we've conned ourselves into thinking that we could skip prerequisite A and proceed directly to B. Now, instead of undoing our mistake and dropping the class, we don't do the assignments on time and tell ourselves that any old grade will be fine in light of how little we did to earn it.

3. **I'm afraid of failing.** This is a classic excuse for pro-crastinating. We're actually afraid to try, to get ego-invested in hoping we'll succeed, only to find out that the ordeal wasn't worth our time or trouble. Of course, without effort we're almost guaranteed we will fail, so not trying isn't a solution.

4. **I may succeed now, but I'll fail later when more is expected of me.** This is called *fear of success*, also known as *fear of future failure*. It springs from the idea that "I'm not good enough and I don't deserve enduring success. So why start to succeed when I know I'll let everybody down later, including myself?" People put off mating, dating, starting families, and other big life events be-cause of this concern that when more is expected, less will be delivered.

5. **I'm so bored with this!** For generations, media pun-dits have warned that our gadgets, TVs, and now our smartphones and other devices, are ruining the ability of people to focus on more important matters and to con-centrate in general. Author Ray Bradbury envisioned this craving for constant stimulation in his book *Fahrenheit 451,* where screens became ubiquitous. Devices insisted on having real-time interactions with viewers. When you can tap an almost limitless database of diverting articles, websites, movies, TV shows, and music, how can "bor-ing" projects compete?

What most of these excuses have in common is that the procrastinator is unable to contentedly postpone gratification. That is, people don't want to sacrifice the "now" in pursuit of a "later" that is greater.

I earned five college degrees, a BA, MA, PhD, JD, and MBA. I don't really want to dwell on the number of years I put in, but let's say I have more time invested in college and grad-school courses than the average American has in his or her total education.

A friend of mine from karate, a very smart fellow interested in self-improvement, asked me how I found the time to study for and complete my law degree and then pass the notoriously tough bar exam on the first try. I also got through it while maintaining a consulting practice.

"I stopped watching TV," I replied.

I explained that the average person watches five hours or more of programming each day. It's pleasant and engaging, but it doesn't advance them in any way.

I decided to simply reallocate that time.

I traded instant gratification for long-term gratification.

And I have to admit, much of law school and the sacrifice it entailed was painful. Taking "Secured Transactions" was less enjoyable than any sports event I could have dialed in on my two hundred–plus cable channels.

But I got to meet and chat with famous sports agents that were alumni of my law school. I learned more about the backstage management of sports than I could have ever learned glued to a tube.

What does this have to do with the "game of inches" that I've been alluding to?

Becoming a lawyer seems to involve going through a daunting gauntlet. You have to apply and be accepted to schools, and to apply you usually have to have completed a BA or BS degree. Plus, you have to have taken and done pretty well on the LSAT—the Law School Admissions Test.

You need recommendations from prior teachers and character references. This entails *asking*, which many people find embarrassing or distasteful.

And of course, day to day there are all of those classes you must attend—no way around it—if you want to qualify to sit for the bar exam three or four years down the road.

And you can rule out going on leisurely vacations and doing the "normal" things "civilians" do. Lots of marriages go on the rocks because of the demands placed on law students.

You can understand why someone would procrastinate about going to law school or to any grad school or even college, right? There are lots and lots of things to do, and prolonged formal education seems without end.

At least at the beginning, it does.

BUT IT IS FINITE! There is an end to it, and you can get there if you don't stumble over the fact that the terminus seems so very far away.

There is this joke you hear when you're entertaining the idea of going to law school:

"Do you know how old you'll be by the time you become a lawyer?" The answer is: "The exact same age I'll be if I don't."

But there is one fact that procrastinators conceal from themselves. Sure, goals and tasks can seem overwhelming, if you insist on seeing them as all-or-nothing, must-do-right-away accomplishments.

Again, most people are very good FINISHERS. but LOUSY STARTERS. Once they are under way with something, they tend to complete it.

This is because they can monitor their progress after they have gotten under way. Getting under way is the trick, for most.

Sure, there seem to be exceptions. You might have heard horror stories about doctoral candidates that never finish their dissertations. Instead of seizing those sheepskins that read "Doctor So-and-So," they live in agony with the idea that they'll never earn that ultimate academic distinction (as many see it).

Certainly they have a problem with finishing, correct? Yes, it would seem so. But if you look closely, even finishing has a beginning, a middle, and an end.

Those stuck in this way have not BEGUN to FINISH.

There is a way to go back to their projects and to find an *entry point*, which is exactly what every procrastinator should do with an undone task.

This step or inch taken may be so obvious that it is overlooked.

Once I happened across an article about getting things done. It was buried in the literature about time management.

I loved its first point, step number one, and I'll share it with you. It said:

FIRST, CLEAR OFF ENOUGH SPACE.

I must admit that as I write these words, my desk is a mess!

But there is enough space for my keyboard and screen, so I'm chugging along nonetheless.

Many of us are stuck in the muck of inactivity and procrastination because we haven't created a vacuum through which that initial effort can enter.

This has become apparent to me when I have consulted for other companies. I'm provided with a spare desk, office, or conference room. My digs are temporary, and they typically need to be folded up like a tent at the end of the working day.

Thus I start with enough space and I end with enough space. The setting simply won't let me be a pack rat.

Look around your workspace. Is there enough? Is it cluttered? Your first order of business is clearing it off.

Is that too much to ask? Here's where an inch will be huge. Do as I'm doing right now.

I just tossed into the trash a $1-off coupon for organic milk. I buy the stuff, but not at the store the coupon came from. They charge two or three dollars more than the store where I buy my organics.

So I know this coupon is really worthless, because even using it, I'll still overpay.

Tossing that one was easy.

Let's find another no-brainer to cast away. Ah, junk mail and never-to-be-used business-reply envelopes. Goodbye!

Another coupon—this time two bucks off for an obscure wine that I'll never buy.

You get the point.

There's more to do, but now I have momentum. I can actually see the oak finish of this beautiful antique roll-top desk. I'm making progress!

My desk is completely overgrown with extraneous junk, so the task of cleaning it seems daunting. But after just a few tossed items, I can envision the finishing line: a clean desktop.

This is the path to overcoming procrastination of all kinds. You might procrastinate because of low self-esteem, or because you are bored, or because you are a pleasure seeker, or for a reason I haven't mentioned.

Lots of problems can lead to this time trap. But there is a universal solvent, and that is taking ONE SMALL ACTION toward a goal.

Let me add a tip that will help you to START. Be willing to do that one little thing BADLY.

Perfectionism, it is widely pointed out, leads to procrastination. Perfectionists insist that everything be just right before starting or leaving a task. All the ducks need to be in a row, everything must be organized and anticipated down to the most miniscule and trivial detail.

Having a perfectionist's sensibilities will almost ensure that you'll accomplish far less than everyone else.

But you will have a built-in excuse for your relative lack of accomplishment: you have HIGH STANDARDS!

I'm here to advise you to lower them, and, in the worst cases of procrastination, to lower them dramatically.

Perfectionists are not willing to risk doing things badly. But underperforming is practically inevitable, especially if you are a novice at something.

Every lawyer and brain surgeon has had a first client or a first patient. I know, you're thinking, "Please, don't let me be that person!"

Anyway, there is a first time for everything, but if you won't permit yourself to be a beginner, you'll never evolve into being a master of that task or skill. You absolutely must take the risk that your first attempt may be off the mark slightly, or may even be grossly ineffective.

If you're a new pilot, you'll take the controls while a skilled instructor sits in the cockpit next to you. You can only go so far astray in that situation.

But if you have an inflated sense of self-importance and you want to be as flawless in piloting as that instructor your first time out, you'll procrastinate and possibly never allow yourself to take the controls.

You must permit yourself to fail.

Starting modestly can help, making your progress a game of inches.

I ran into a friend of mine at a social gathering. He invited me to attend a class at a martial-arts school where he had been rising through the ranks for about four years.

I went on a Sunday afternoon. My pal, along with five or six others, marched down the mat quickly, throwing in coordinated action kicks and hand strikes so quickly that it looked like a bam-bam martial-arts ballet.

Wow, they were good!

I couldn't imagine how one could command one's body that way. It had to take years, I thought.

I signed up, and took classes and private training sessions. About a month into my training, a car hit me as I walked from my office to have lunch at a nearby mall. That set my training back a little while.

Clumsy as I felt myself to be, I used the inch-by-inch philosophy. In fact, after a point, I didn't want to show off and seem advanced. I just did what I was told, again and again.

And do you know what happened? About eight years later, I became a black belt.

I need to put this achievement into perspective. Only nineteen other students had reached black belt in thirty-two years at my school. Over 10,000 students came and went in that time. My black belt was a rare achievement, and I don't mind saying I got really good at this art.

I taught at the same dojo and helped others. But my pal, the one that had introduced me, never went beyond green belt. He skipped out on advanced green, and on three levels of the exacting brown belt level, and of course he never got close to black belt.

Yet when I first saw him participating, he seemed like a deity. How did I not only meet his capabilities, but also go on to significantly surpass him?

Inch by inch is the answer.

I showed up. I trained. I trusted that I would be one of the last candidates standing. And I was.

What's interesting is the fact that martial arts always fascinated me. I'd read plenty of books on the subject. But I didn't take a single class until my friend invited me to watch his.

You could say I was procrastinating.

But watching that first class, moving a single inch toward the goal, was the first step in what Confucius might have called a journey of a thousand leagues.

Procrastinators fear that the end is so far away that they'll never live to see it.

But it arrives so much faster after we have taken that one-inch step!

Do something that isn't grandiose but rather that is so modest and unambitious as to seem piddling and trivial.

Start there.

In our following sections, I'll show that this incremental approach is just what the doctor ordered to overcome stage fright, phone, fear, and writer's block, as well as other afflictions that are shooing success away from your doorstep.

2

Finding a Great Partner

In the Beatles song "Eleanor Rigby," there is a tear-jerking refrain: "All the lonely people / Where do they all come from? / All the lonely people / Where do they all belong?"

The quest for a great partner, a husband, wife, boyfriend, girlfriend, or even just a wonderful pal, seems to be filled with inevitable joys and sorrows. It is the sorrow part that discourages millions of people from making the journey altogether.

While there may be no perfect way to keep our fragile hearts from breaking, we can transform ourselves into better navigators of the partner-searching enterprise.

We can overcome the negative inertia that grips people who have abandoned the challenge, who are shrinking away from sharing life's ups and downs with a co-pilot.

Yesterday I spotted a used bookstore near the school where my daughters are taking ballet lessons. I had some extra time before their classes concluded, so I walked in.

I asked where the business and how-to sections were

located, but with winces the clerks told me that the section had been moved to another store they owned about a mile away.

I was walking, so that was out of bounds for me. I decided to browse anyway. They had thousands of volumes on display, and I found a section titled "Self-Improvement."

"Perfect," I thought, and I browsed the titles. I found a promising one: *Why Be an Imitation When You Were Born an Original?*

Leafing through it, I was impressed with the table of contents, and, like some of my early books, it wasn't a huge opus, but was rather compact.

I sat in an overstuffed chair and started reading. Bouncing from chapter to chapter, I pretty much finished the book, and by that time I needed to pick up some groceries and the girls.

Suddenly I found myself in a good mood. One of the author's points echoed the advice of John Wesley, founder of Methodism, to leave people you meet better off than you found them, to somehow add value to their lives.

Apparently that thought put a smile on my lips. As I walked to the grocery store, someone smiled back at me. That made me grin even more, because I recognized the truth in the adage "You get back what you send out."

Inside the market, much the same story unfolded. Except for one woman who wore a scowl, people were unusually friendly toward me. One person offered me her spot in the checkout line, for no apparent reason. Another lady started a conversation with me.

I have to tell you that this is unusual. Ordinarily I go about my personal business, I suppose, as if it were a business. And I probably wear a facial expression to match that attitude.

But the book made me lighten up. And I guess that glow felt good to other people, who, in their respective ways, basked in it.

What could have been an exasperating delay in the rush-hour traffic of stalled shopping carts became a small pleasure, not just for me, but for others as well.

What does this episode have to do with mating, dating, romance, and bonding with other people?

Everything!

I was once speaking with a prominent psychiatrist. As is my habit when I encounter accomplished people in any field, I try to formulate a perfect question. This is a question that elicits just the information I want or need. It is also well-crafted enough to be customized to the person I'm chatting with.

It is also enjoyable for that person to answer. Typically, you know you've done it when someone responds, with a grin, "That's a really good question!"

For instance, I was standing at a red light at the corner of Beverly Drive and Wilshire Boulevard in Beverly Hills when famous science-fiction author Ray Bradbury walked up to my right.

I asked him, "Mr. Bradbury, I've often wondered what you thought of François Truffaut's rendering of your book *Fahrenheit 451*."

He replied, "It brought me to tears."

"Me too," I said, moved that he had been touched by the film in exactly the same way that I had.

To go back to my conversation with the psychiatrist, I asked him, "What is the best way to get other people to like you?"

Without hesitating, he said, "Like them FIRST."

A glib reading of his reply would make this seem as if it came straight out of Dale Carnegie's *How to Win Friends and Influence People.*

There is a similarity, but what the psychiatrist was saying is different. Showing people you like them is exceedingly impressive.

Consider it for a moment. When we feel someone likes us, we immediately think they have great taste in people, correct? We're pretty cool, they see it, and they are cool for seeing it.

And one of the most important laws of attraction kicks in. We tend to reciprocate when someone does something nice for us.

If the nice thing they did was to like us, reciprocating is simply a matter of liking them back.

But what do we normally do if we are unaware of the doctor's suggestion? We wait, and wait, and wait for other people to show us first that they approve of us.

If they don't let on that they do, even if we like them, we may withhold our signs of liking them.

By doing so, we delay and perhaps discourage altogether the exchanging of approval gestures that tell us we're at the beginning of a good relationship.

Let's turn to the animal world for a moment.

I decided it was time to get a dog. I had never had one growing up, and finally, when I was in my first house and I could do as I pleased, I felt it was the right time to take action.

Instead of purchasing a dog from a pet store, I decided to adopt. I learned there was an adoption event at a ranch about fifteen miles from me, so I trekked over and looked around.

There were some kennels set up, and most people focused on those dogs. I did too, but I noticed there was a dog tied to a corral post that seemed to be barking at me as I headed toward the exit.

Insistent on getting my attention, this Doberman, who was beautiful but not what I was looking for, barked less as I approached her.

Gingerly, I stood in front of her and slowly extended my hand. And what she did next totally stopped me in my tracks.

She leaned up against me, putting most of her weight on my leg.

The signal I got from this was, "You're mine, big guy. Take me home!"

And that's what happened. I melted after she melted. She showed me she liked me.

After that moment, it was all over. I needed to look no farther.

Shana turned out to be a wonder dog, adept at fetching Frisbees and tennis balls, and never missing a step-off lead in cadence with me when we jogged for miles around the neighborhood. People would marvel when they saw her.

After we were together for about six years, when Shana was about ten years old (from what I could surmise), she hurriedly trotted downstairs and laid her head on my feet, and then peacefully took her last breath.

Relationships start, quite often, inch by inch. Putting a smile on our faces is a journey of even less than an inch, measured by how much our lips need to move.

What is Mona Lisa's smile? An eighth of an inch? A quarter?

A smile not only signals that we like someone, but sends innumerable signals about us. Smiles can speak volumes about how we feel about ourselves.

If I'm out of sorts, if I feel dejected, if I'm not meeting my goals in life, don't expect to see me smiling. And I can tell you something else.

If I'm not smiling, I'm not very attractive at that moment. Remember that one woman at the market that I noticed, the one wearing a scowl?

My first impression was, "What wrong with her?" My second was, "Stay away from her!"

My third was, "Is it me? Is my sweater dirty? Does she dislike me for some reason?"

My fourth was, "It has to be her. No one else is giving me the stink eye!"

Consider these reactions. Which one is telling me, "Hey, I'd really like to get to know her?"

Exactly. If the scowling person wanted anything from me, say, to cut in line or to have me give her the right of way as we reached for some vegetables, do you think I would yield?

I might, out of sheer politeness, or out of fear of reprisal. But it's not likely, correct?

People that wear gentle smiles are either great actors or super-phonies—or they're something else, something more positive.

They could actually be HAPPY at that moment. That is a very attractive quality, happiness.

Well-balanced, nice folks are attracted to happy people. They feel safe in their presence. Being somewhat happy themselves, they can relate.

It isn't a huge leap to feel, at least unconsciously, "We could be happy together!"

People are imitators. We are inclined to mirror people's emotions back to them. If they seem open and welcoming, like a warm host at a party, we loosen up and warm up ourselves.

If they signal that we've arrived too soon, or if they've just had an argument with their mates, we recoil and take on their negativity, or at least we become tentative and less demonstrative.

Unless we are wired badly (or at least differently), we move toward the smiles and away from the scowls.

There are exceptions.

I was doing a consulting project for a Wall Street firm. I was happy to be there, not so much at the firm, but in New York City.

I had my wife and four-month-old daughter with me. We took a big suite for the week at the Waldorf Tower, and were surrounded by lavish oil paintings and the accoutrements of success and comfort.

I knew they were going to have a blast while I was off at work. They were set to visit the Metropolitan Museum of Art, to stroll in the park, and to have lots of fun adventures together.

And I was being paid to do what I do best: to train people to be more effective at what they do. I thought all was going swimmingly, but then my contact took me aside.

He said I looked too happy. I smiled too much. People at that Wall Street firm wore dour masks that were their game faces as they competed hard, with the goal of beating the world into submission.

Well, I was happy; that's true. It showed, and so what? I was paid well, and my family was having a great vacation, and we have the pictures to prove it!

Remembering all of this, I'm still smiling!

The inch-by-inch approach to interpersonal bonding tells you to start modestly. You do what is in your power to do to say, "I'm open to having a meaningful relationship."

Openness is communicated through self-disclosure, when we reveal tidbits of information about ourselves.

If you want to advance a relationship, it almost always entails the sharing of details with others. Here's why it is crucial.

By opening up, we make ourselves vulnerable. People can take the information we disclose and make jokes at our expense. They can trivialize what we have said is important to us. They can disagree strongly with our opinions. They can create distance, not intimacy.

All of which can sting and make us regret that we tried to open up in the first place.

But at the same time, by opening ourselves, other people can peer into our souls and find profound reasons to bond with us. They can identify with our experiences, our backgrounds, our hopes and dreams.

They can see themselves in us, and this is intoxicating and redeeming. They may have believed that no one else shared their views or goals, and they may feel great relief at discovering a kindred spirit.

Please don't get the idea that opening up means over-sharing or doing a massive personal-data dump. Sure, a first date could have you both talking well into the night about details of your personal lives, but this will be facilitated through making modest and measured disclosures at first.

That question that inhibits most of us—"Can I trust this person with my secrets?"—is still a pertinent issue when we don't know someone. But here's the rub, as Shakespeare might have put it.

We will never know if we can trust people until we trust them with some detail or secret and then see what they do with it!

So begin with small disclosures. If you like certain foods, or you are a good chef, say so. Put that small fact out there.

You have a pet peeve? Well, if it is going to be a deal-killer when it comes to forming or sustaining a relationship, maybe you should mention it at some point.

Inch by inch, you'll get to know each other, and will like what you come to discover, or not.

But it is all good practice. This is what you should tell yourself.

There is a commercial enterprise that plays match-maker to busy professionals. I really don't know anything about it except its name, which I think is great: "It's Just Lunch."

This business name says it all. Getting together with someone, at least initially, isn't about doing the wedding planning on the first date. Far from it—it is about having a low-risk encounter.

You see someone you like, and you start a conversation, about anything.

"Well, we're finally getting some rain!" will do the trick.

Or you can be bolder.

"Have you voted yet?"

Admittedly, these are imperfect gambits, but they are conversation starters. And that's exactly the point: to start!

But what if you're rejected? What if they fail to respond or give you the cold shoulder or show you their encircled ring finger?

What then? It's no big deal. Don't take it personally.

Scratch it up to experience. You tried.

I studied with Dr. Albert Ellis, who is considered one of the top five modern influences in psychology. Ellis is the father of what has come to be known as rational emotive behavior therapy (REBT). I'll sum it up for you.

REBT says that few reactions we get from other people are awful. Instead it is our interpretation of these reactions that really upsets us. We can choose a different reaction and thereby control our emotions.

Ellis was not a Lothario by any means. He had severe illnesses as a child that confined him to his house. But he wanted to date and mate, so he had to get out of his shell.

He decided to spend a lot of time at the Brooklyn Botanic Garden. To overcome his shyness and lack of self-confidence, he started conversations with one hundred women. Not all in one day, mind you; this was a long-term project.

Did he get a date? I'm not sure, but he did learn something crucial that informed his development of REBT.

By repeatedly doing what you fear, by doing your "homework," as he labeled it, you will overcome that fear.

After a while, he became inured to starting conversations with strangers and to being rejected. He kept going. He got so many nonresponses and rejections that he conquered them all.

Each person he spoke to was just a single inch, to put it in our terms.

And thus the inch-by-inch philosophy merges into what I call the Law of Large Numbers. This is also the title of one of my best-selling audio seminars, and it conveys this truth:

If you do enough of anything, you will succeed. If you do more than that, you will grow wealthy. And if you go far beyond that amount of repeated activity, you'll become a legend.

Ellis proved to himself the truth in the ancient philosopher Epictetus's aphorism: "What upsets people is not things themselves but their judgments about the things"

You can be rejected a hundred times or more, and still succeed. Indeed, it may require 200 or 500 or 1000 setbacks until you overcome the impediment.

Michael Jordan is still considered one of the best athletes ever to play professional basketball. But his journey to the top was pockmarked by failure after failure. He recalls:

"I've missed more than 9000 shots in my career. I've lost almost 300 games. Twenty-six times, I've been trusted to take the game winning shot and missed. I've failed over and over and over again in my life. And that is why I succeed."

What does this have to do with finding a great partner? You have to show up at each encounter, ready to play. You need to keep asking for the ball and taking shots when opportunities are presented to you.

It is all of these baby steps, combined and repeated, that make the difference between a champion and an also-ran.

Smiling leads to talking. Talking leads to more talking and to dating. Dating leads to bonding and to intimacy.

Moments become hours, and days become months and years, and this is the way relationships form and succeed.

But they all start inch by inch.

3

Developing High-Value Relationships

You see it everywhere: the ability to forge great relationships is a big secret to success. Employment ads, whether they're seeking to hire the most junior, entry-level persons or the most exalted CEOs, call on applicants to demonstrate they have the ability to get others to bond with them, to willingly come under their spells.

There is a memorable sequence in what has been considered the best movie of all time: *The Godfather*.

Bonasera, an ordinary mortician, comes to ask Don Vito Corleone, the Godfather, for help. Bonasera's daughter has been mercilessly abused, her honor and virtue violated. Her visibly shaken papa wants vengeance.

The Godfather doesn't instantly grant the man his wish. He reminds the supplicant that he was too proud to accept the Godfather's help in the past; he felt it beneath him. Don Corleone says, "I understand. You found paradise in America, you had a good trade, you made a good living. The police protected you; and there were courts of law. And you didn't need a friend like me. But now you come to me, and you say: 'Don Corleone, give me justice.' But you don't ask with respect. You don't offer friendship. You don't even think to call me Godfather. Instead, you come into my house on the day my daughter is to be married, and you ask me to do murder for money."

"I ask for justice," Bonasera replies.

"That is not justice; your daughter is still alive."

"Then they can suffer, as she suffers," says Bonasera. "How much shall I pay you?"

Don Corleone turns his back on him and says, "Bonasera, Bonasera. What have I ever done to make you treat me so disrespectfully? Had you come to me in friendship, then this scum that ruined your daughter would be suffering this very day. And that by chance if an honest man such as yourself should make enemies, then they would become my enemies. And then they would fear you."

Bonasera then asks for the Godfather's friendship, to which he famously replies: "Good. Someday, and that day may never come, I'll call upon you to do a service for me. But until that day—accept this justice as a gift on my daughter's wedding day."

This is the setup for the other shoe to drop later, when the Godfather seeks the mortician's help in his hour of grief and profound need.

Favors given and favors returned are one way that effective relationships work. It's known as reciprocity, and the saying that aptly describes it is "One hand washes the other."

Yet the Godfather's example is both instructive and subtle. He tenders his help and refers to it as a "gift" on his daughter's wedding day. There are some important subtexts to this statement.

Because of his vast power, the Godfather is somewhat duty-bound to provide his help, especially on a jubilant day such as that of his daughter's wedding. It is clever of him to characterize his intention to fulfill the mortician's request as a gift.

Does a gift need to be requited by a gift from the recipient? Not necessarily, but one indication that we have a relationship with someone else is that there is a reciprocal exchange, some give-and-take.

As the Godfather points out, "that day may never come." But, he is implying, "If it comes, you, Mr. Bonasera, have an obligation to pay me back. If and when I need you, you will be there for me. That's the deal."

Reciprocal exchanges can happen immediately. Most commercial transactions are like this. You go to a gas station and insert your card into the slot, and you can pump gas into your car.

Does this mean you have a relationship with that pump or with that gas station? I don't think so, because you are under no obligation to keep buying gasoline there.

In the *Godfather* example, there was a significant gap in time between doing the favor for the mortician and then seeking a favor from him. That type of longer-term commitment signals the presence of a relationship, because there is a carried-over value.

A neighbor comes to you and says, "I almost bought your house, but I was too late in making an offer. If you ever decide to sell, would you please let me know first? I'll buy it directly from you, and you'll save on paying a realtor's commission."

Do you have a duty to follow through when you're thinking of selling? It depends on whether that person is a good neighbor—someone who picks up your newspapers and rolls your trash to the street when you are out of town.

Did that neighbor build rapport with you, inch by inch, or come to you all of a sudden out of nowhere, as the mortician did with the Godfather? Isn't this what the Godfather complained about—the lack of inch-by-inch friendship building?

Crass as it may seem, sometimes I use a banking metaphor to describe how relationships build. If we make a habit of depositing funds in someone's emotional "bank," then this gives rise to a reasonable expectation that we'll be able to make withdrawals from their bank when our need arises.

"Had you been my friend," the Godfather explained, he would have been happier about granting the mortician's favor. No deposits, no withdrawals allowed. Lucky you asked on the occasion of my daughter's wedding!

The smart way to build high-value relationships is not to insist on immediate return of value for value. We may seek this in a negotiation, and we may be correct in expecting a concurrent exchange to happen. But the wise relationship builder "opens an account" with someone by making a deposit first.

Of course, much of relationship building can be traced to getting other people to like us. You can be the greatest expert at something, possessing a most needed skill, yet if you aren't also likeable, to some degree, you'll stymie yourself professionally and socially.

One of my first communication professors, a silver-haired former captain in the Navy and a retired contract instructor with Dale Carnegie, was fond of putting it this way: "Find something you like or admire in some-one else, and compliment them for it."

People will treasure you if you sincerely praise them, especially for a quality they never knew they possessed.

4

The Importance of Slowing Down

Who sets the pace of your life? Is it you? Or is it someone else?

I remember being in karate and having an interesting chat on the mat with my instructor.

He said, "What are you waiting for? Why aren't you moving faster?"

I replied, "I'm pacing myself, ramping up to full speed."

In other words, I had my own internalized idea of how much intensity and output I should be producing in terms of kicks and blocks and hand strikes and overall body movements.

He had another.

Of course, I took his point to heart.

Instructors ran a drill to get us to emit the right quantum of focus and force. They would shout a number from one to three, and we had to calibrate our responses with a hand strike or a kick or a flurry.

"Three!" signified an all-out assault on our target, holding nothing back. Imagine meeting a life-or-death threat, someone wielding a knife or a gun, and you're at level three. Level one was far more restrained. Perhaps someone aggressively shoves you, and you feel you have to respond with force without making things worse.

And of course level two was something in between. It's not life or death, but say two miscreants have attacked you at the same time.

The purpose of this calibration drill was to implant the understanding that different provocations and circumstances required measured results. A slight threat needs to be met with a moderate response, sufficient to the provocation but not too much.

They say baby rattlesnakes are the worst because they don't measure the amount of venom in their bites. It's all or nothing, and this is much the way non–martial artists address threats.

Small provocations thus elicit disproportionate reactions, and this means that encounters quickly spiral out of control. The result is someone could be killed, when the proper response would have done much less damage with minor consequences.

The law in many civilized countries reflects the idea that self-defense is permitted, but you cannot exceed an amount of force that is proportionate to the provocation. If someone slaps you in the face, you can't justify bashing the person into a pulp with a baseball bat. You can stop the threat with less force, although this is often easier said than done.

In my martial-arts training, I was taught to try to slow conflicts down for the express purpose of retaining control. Part of this process involves detecting when someone else is about to fly off the handle, so that you can leave the scene or diffuse the threat with words or by allowing the person more space.

You've heard that some folks do a "slow burn" emotionally. They quietly seethe or ruminate before lashing out at others. You can feel their hostility and read certain nonverbal cues, and you can respond accordingly.

This idea of slowing reality is something that great athletes do as a matter of course. Professional baseball batters—and here I'm referring to those that stand out year after year—are able to see the ball differently than average players. They can spot the rotation of the seams of the baseball, tipping them off to the type of pitch that is hurling toward them at 70 to 105 miles per hour. Thus they garner a split second of extra decision time as to whether they should swing or not, where they angle their swing, and how hard they should swing.

But there is something that these great professionals know that enables them to make these game-winning and career-boosting adjustments. They know they can slow time down in this particular way.

Controlling our time is essential in creating successful results.

I'm going to refer to these things separately and at greater length, but overcoming stage fright, phone fear, writing anxiety, and other forms of communication apprehension all benefit from making the clock your friend.

For example, last week I delivered a keynote speech before an audience of four hundred professionals, very bright people, who work in the area of data mining. I had set the date with the conference director eleven months beforehand.

That meant I had plenty of time to worry about writing and delivering that speech. I'm a professional speaker and a best-selling author, so you might think that stage fright and writing anxiety are things of the past for me, that I overcame them long ago.

Not so. They still bother me, a little. And this tension is actually good, because it drives me to excel, to prepare, and to make sure I do well.

What I have learned to do is to postpone my worries until it is too late to worry.

Remember, I had about eleven months in which I could have dreaded delivering that talk. But I told myself to wait.

I knew I would start writing my speech about four weeks before the occasion. In the final week, I'd put on the finishing touches and be 100 percent prepared as I stepped up to the podium.

A funny thing happened. My association contact started sending me reminders, checking with me about my microphone requirements and such, and she referred to the date as coming up "next week."

I'd thought it was two weeks away. But I found that I had one less week to prepare and to worry!

I needed to accelerate my progress, and fortunately I had the spare time to tackle the task immediately.

By that point I was too busy writing to have any time left over for worrying. Plus, the shorter calendar-to-event time simply denied me the opportunity to indulge in wasteful worry.

For that, I was grateful.

Worry will take up all of the time you allow for it. When you learn to postpone the worry, you do yourself a huge favor, releasing your attention so you can accomplish other things.

Choosing how you use your time is an essential tool of success.

Earlier I implied that there are two choices we all have: (1) we can yield control of our time to others; or (2) we can retain it for ourselves.

To do things inch by inch presupposes that we can choose to do things slowly, that there aren't external forces pushing us to make yard-by-yard progress.

Let's go back to my association contact. Her reminders had a slightly anxious tone to them. As the date of her convention approached, naturally she grew nervous. Part of the subtext of her missives to me was aimed at being reassured that my program would progress smoothly, and that I was going to meet my commitment.

I responded to her notes quickly and confidently, providing her with a level of comfort that enabled her to reduce her performance anxiety with regard to the convention she was overseeing.

It would have been easy to mirror her anxiety back to her, and thus to escalate it. That, in turn, would have been lasered back to me, multiplied in intensity. And we could have disoriented each other, making us bring a bundle of nerves to the event.

This destructive mirroring of worry and anxiety induces us to lose valuable time and to dissipate huge stores of energy that can be deployed into productive pursuits.

I told myself, "Her concern is natural. She doesn't know how effective I am as a speaker: I do."

Calming her calmed me down.

Choosing the pace of your working day, your career, and your life is essential to being happy. If you hand over this responsibility to others, such as managers and bosses, you'll probably be kept busy. That may be a benefit to you—enabling you to avoid responsibility for your time.

I am the opposite way. I don't like being pushed, regulated, or dictated to. I have chosen a certain inch-by-inch approach to my life, as my father before me did in his.

He told me a story about being asked to deliver a speech before his fellow sales engineers at a big company. He was unexpectedly frank. Here's what he said:

"Ladies and gentlemen, see that clock on the wall? It is meaningless, and I urge you to ignore it. This is what I do, and this is why I'm so successful and I'm the top seller here."

What did he mean? He continued, "The early bird gets the worm, but that's all he gets. I'm a night owl, so I sleep late, getting up around 9. By 10 or 10:30 I have a leisurely breakfast out, and then I start my selling day feeling great. I may visit a client or a prospect that afternoon and possibly two. But if I don't feel like selling, I don't push myself to do it, because if I feel bad, I won't sell anyone anyway. That's my success secret."

Dad refused to be pushed into anything. His paychecks were issued by companies at which he officially toiled as an employee, but first and foremost he worked for himself.

He owned the clock. And he sold inch by inch, and this is the way he rose to the top and stayed there, while everyone else was preaching the yard-by-yard approach without coming close to his achievements.

If you want to accelerate your progress, often it pays to slow down.

Or as some people put it, "When the going gets tough, the tough go shopping!"

They distract themselves for a while, or they purposely retool by taking continuing education classes, or by doing self-study.

I have found that it is far easier and more productive to do two major activities at once instead of one. I worked my way through college and through graduate school.

In practical terms, I had no choice. I needed to support myself and to make my way in the world.

But this was a huge blessing in disguise. I needed to take work seriously. Otherwise I'd be fired and wouldn't be able to pay my rent. I had to do well in school so I could earn my degrees and advance my level of contribution.

But neither activity took on undue importance in my mind. When work became a slog, schooling perked up, and my classes uplifted my spirits.

The same thing applied to school. When my courses

were tough, I found that achieving on my job lightened my spirits.

Inch-by-inch progress in school and at work multiplied, and I racked up huge successes incrementally.

By slowing down, I got faster at everything.

I've come to appreciate how I work best, and I suggest you listen to your inner voices to determine this for yourself.

My dad criticized early-bird thinking, noting he was a night owl. He was taking about circadian rhythms, the biological periods of work and rest that feel natural to us. He observed these rhythms in himself and then built his life around them. He knew he wasn't any good to anyone without sufficient sleep. And it would have been a disaster if he had to start his working day at, say, 6 or 7 in the morning.

In college, when I dispatched taxis on weekends, I saw similarities in many of our drivers. Some thrived on the night shift, others early in the morning, and a few in between. Because we had to staff twenty-four hours every day, this divergence in circadian rhythms benefitted everyone that listened to and accepted them.

Personal-productivity gurus issue a uniform instruction to those that want to accomplish more: "Know thy time." This often means keeping a time log or diary, into which you post notes regarding where you time goes and how you spend it.

This is a good inch-by-inch idea. By seeing the seepage points, where time is evaporating or out of control, or is simply being wasted, you can make minor adjustments and reap big results.

A salesperson who can make just one more phone call a day, five days week, or about twenty-four more outreaches a month, may be able to close one more deal during that time. If a deal is worth $1000 in commissions, this is $12,000 per year. That could mean a boost to their overall income by several percentage points, enabling them to take better vacations or to live far more comfortably.

You can accomplish mighty things though a small improvement here and there with regard to time management.

A writer who can simply add two hundred words each day to a text can compose a 50,000-word book in less than a year!

Liberating just one hour per day, or less, can help you accomplish this amazing task.

Slow down, listen to your biorhythms, and know thy time. You'll accomplish far more and feel far better about it!

Inch by inch, it's a cinch.

5

How to Get Unstuck

Highway 198 in central California winds for about fifty miles from Interstate 5, the trucker's roadway of choice, to the 101, which parallels the Pacific coastline.

It's a haunted path, casting dark shadows through its silted canyons. You don't want to drive it at night, because its single-lane bridges and incessant switchbacks require 100 percent of your attention even in broad daylight. Staying on the road is hard work in the best of conditions.

But that serpentine is still a useful shortcut from I-5, the "Autobahn," as Californians refer to it, to the more scenic and languid 101.

I was traversing 198 in the late autumn when a sudden thunderstorm came on. Visibility was practically zero. At one point I pulled over to the shoulder to wait out the deluge.

As the skies cleared and the rainfall stuttered to a drizzle, I restarted the engine without difficulty. But I made no forward progress. My wheels spun in the mud, and the rear wheels settled into a depression.

Checking out what happened, I suddenly realized what the last road sign meant: *Soft Shoulder*. When you leave the pavement as I did, you move onto a substance that acts like quicksand. Your wheels can get swallowed if that shoulder is wet, and certainly if it is super-saturated, which the turf had very much become.

My cell phone was receptionless. I couldn't call for help. Literally, I was stuck in the middle of nowhere, in one of the few trafficless places in California.

It was approaching 3:45. The gray late afternoon light would soon be turning to stark black. I was going to spend a freezing cold night in the car. I felt like a sitting duck for any dangers that could be in store.

Forcing the worst-case scenarios from my mind, I ordered my thoughts to conjure up a solution.

"What do I need?" I asked myself out loud.

"You need a shovel to dig yourself out of this mess," I replied a long minute later.

My self-blaming voice interrupted this rational one-man dialogue. It mocked me :"Soft shoulder! Why doesn't anyone explain what that means? If I had realized the meaning of that phrase, I would have kept at least two wheels on the solid roadway as I pulled over.

"That sign, that bloody sign," my self-blaming voice repeated.

Then it hit me.

Exactly! That triangular sign can serve as a shovel!

Instantly I trekked back to where I had seen it, about a hundred feet away. Urgently and relentlessly, I wriggled the signpost back and forth. Initially it resisted my efforts.

At first I made no progress, but as my hands turned red and swelled, the sign began to budge. About fifteen minutes later, at about 4:15, I pulled it out of the ground and started to frantically shovel the mud from beneath my back wheels.

Filthy, but committed to conquering this problem I had created, I started the engine and maneuvered the wheels back to the road, and we continued our trip.

Within twenty minutes, it was completely dark, but we had made it to the 101. I don't think I've ever been more grateful to see other headlights in my life!

Whenever I'm stuck and I don't know what to do, I purposely summon to mind this astonishing episode. It contains several hints for extricating yourself from the stickiest situations.

Ask: Can someone else help me? No, the auto club is out of phone range, and all I see is vacant land behind an endless barbed wire fence.

Ask: What do I need to fix this problem? What would be ideal? In my case the answer was, a shovel. But I can't pop the truck and find what I need. What's the next best thing? What can serve as a shovel?

Ask: Where am I going to get a shovel? I must find something outside. What's here that I can use to improvise?

Through these questions, going from problem to solution, my mind served up the answer in the form of a nagging reminder of my stupidity in ignoring the usefulness of the road sign. Aha! It could still be useful. It was designed to help me to avoid this very problem and it can be used NOW to extricate me from this problem.

You may have seen the great movie starring Matt Damon titled *The Martian*. He was alone and marooned on the red planet with a very short supply of food. Clearly, if he stayed stuck where he was, he'd die.

He asked the first question I mentioned above. *Can someone else help me?*

The communications equipment at the base camp had been destroyed. So he had to pluck himself out of his rut.

He asked: *What do I need to fix this problem? What would be ideal?*

The answer was a way of communicating with earth, specifically with mission control, the folks that could send a rescue ship to collect him.

He asked: *Where am I going to find a communication device or something that can work as one?*

He, too, looked around. Recalling prior unmanned missions to Mars, he knew at least that one craft should contain a communication device. If he could reach that remote spot on the planet, dig up the device, and rehabilitate it, he might just have a chance to send a distress signal back to earth.

He faced other daunting obstacles and endured numerous setbacks. But each one he approached using his training as a biologist and scientist.

If you haven't seen the movie, you really should. It was nominated for best picture of the year, and deservedly so. I recall leaving the theater with my family, opening the door to the outdoors, feeling the warm sun on my face, and experiencing a phenomenal sense of relief.

Look at all of the tools we have here on this planet! We can breathe the air! Move about on our own two feet. Communicate in myriad ways! It's all at our fingertips!

Solutions, inch-by-inch solutions, that's what we need. Inch by inch I got that road sign to budge and to leave the ground. Inch by inch I dug the wheels out of the mud onto a solid surface below.

Solutions are everywhere.

We do some our best thinking and inventing when the chips are down. Maybe it's the adrenalin or endorphins that are released into our bloodstreams that are at work. Possibly it is our subconscious, our deeper, survival-oriented minds, that engage, as mine did when I was chastising myself for not heeding that road sign.

It could be that our ancestors receive our SOS signals on a secret emergency frequency and send back helping hints. Angels could be on our shoulders. The history of humanity is replete with examples of how, as historian Arnold Toynbee put it, we have been repeatedly faced with challenges to which we creatively responded.

Don't count us out, especially when we seem to be down for the count. As Buddhist nun Pema Chödrön has written, at any given time "we are just one breath away from enlightenment."

And luckily, if we are resourceful in this life of ours, we can miss a critical road sign, yet use it later to get unstuck and go back on the right path.

6

Managing Your Mind

A fresh rain fell overnight, leaving the backyard in a dewy glow by daybreak. Two seconds into my first cup of coffee, I felt the urge to do some karate in that sparkling light and gusty wind.

Before I put down my cup, several thoughts popped into mind.

I could get electrocuted on a day like this, a bolt of lightning finding the top of my head.

It has to be slippery out there. When I do my kicks I could fall backwards and break my head.

Bet it's cold—sure looks like it.

And then, without another thought, I bolted from chair into the unknown.

It was a great workout, replete with kicks and hand strikes, blocks and parries, and quick movements forward and to the rear. If anyone was watching from across the channel, I'm sure they got their money's worth.

Resuming my coffee, my mood was elevated, to say

the least. I was high, so I decided to watch my thoughts entering and leaving my mind.

I paid special attention to my beliefs. Most of them were stupid, and they could have torpedoed my day. I decided not to let them.

I thought about the blog that I visit and contribute to. "People there have nothing new to say. Time to move on. Find another one? No, it's a waste of time anyway. Let it go."

I felt myself letting it go, along with just about everything else.

One of my daughters' teachers was acting the idiot, flunking her on assignments without just cause. My wife was asking me if she should confront the teacher again.

"Just give her what she asked for and no more," I said in my soothing Zen voice.

Back to my bliss, I asked, "Next?" tempting the demonic inner voices to challenge me by tossing more negative beliefs across my consciousness.

It occurred to me there is a pattern to these limiting beliefs that I announce to myself throughout the day. Many of them are just *outrageous generalizations.*

For example, the weather in the yard wasn't mid-December chilly, as the winds and troubled skies suggested. It was actually warm back there, reminiscent of the tropics, especially of Hawaii after a morning rain shower.

My hunch about chilliness was based on the visual signs I'd been and the fact that we'd had a cold snap for the last week. But just as we see in investment prospectuses, past performance was no guarantee of future performance.

Just because conditions have been a certain way, or at least have seemed so, doesn't mean they'll continue. We can't extrapolate today from yesterday, or tomorrow from today, much as we'd like to.

Generalizations are handy. They are conclusions we draw from evidence we have gathered, deliberately or unconsciously. Because they cover lots of items, we use them to avoid needless complexity.

You're hungry and driving late at night. You see a twenty-four-hour donut shop and salivate. "A donut would be great," you think.

But then you spot a car parked oddly in front, on an angle, and the engine is running. You can see the exhaust gushing from the tailpipe into the crisp air.

Looking inside, you see a rough-looking, leather-clad fellow gesturing to the waif wearing the donut store's cap.

"Is he robbing the place?" you wonder out loud as you start pulling into the lot.

Suddenly you decide to pass on that donut and peel out back into the fast lane.

Yes, he could be a stickup man. Or he could just be pointing impatiently to the items he wants from the glass case.

Either way, you don't want any part of this scene, so you scurry off.

Small gain (happy tummy) or big pain (danger and violence)—it's your choice. It's an approach-avoidance conflict on the surface, and a matter of risk versus reward.

Generally, risk aversion is a more powerful motivation for people than reward attraction. We avoid pain more than we approach pleasure, or most of us do.

As one behavioral scientist put it, "The idea of losing $50 is far more painful than the idea of gaining $50 is pleasurable."

This bias against encountering the unpleasant has survival value. We avoid potential dangers. We live to reach another day, and so do our genes, and we have the hope of passing them on to subsequent generations.

But we also miss opportunities. I see this all the time with my students and trainees in negotiation. For instance, most of them avoid asking their bosses for raises and promotions.

I remind them there's even biblical authority for asking: "Ask and you will receive; seek and you shall find; knock and it will be opened to you."

In everyday language, typically, if you don't ask, you don't get, as I've mentioned in another section.

What's the problem, then? Folks think that asking can boomerang on them. They think they could end up worse off than if they had never asked at all.

"What if she says no?" they blurt out, as if this is one of life's worst possible outcomes.

I reply, "You can ask why." How did they arrive at that no? What is the reasoning? If you get them to respond, you'll at least get some information about your status, or the status of your department and your company. You'll definitely glean some understanding of your boss and her priorities and motivations.

OK, so let's say the worst thing imaginable occurs. Your boss launches into a rant about how undeserving and ungrateful you are, about how you're lucky to even have a job, and if it were up to her, she'd can you right now.

Bad stuff, I agree. I say, it is better to know now, so you can make other plans. The sooner you find a more suitable job and company, the better. You'll be happier, for one thing. You'll be appreciated. And sooner rather than later, your contributions will be acknowledged and rewarded, even if you don't ask.

In your new job, you may also find out an interesting truth. You may find that you didn't desire a raise or a promotion just because you needed or wanted one. You felt something was missing. You felt stuck and unmotivated. You thought money or a new title would help.

But your belief was wrong. You didn't crave those things. You craved recognition and a good boss and company for which to work.

After leaving and finding these things, the money may take on less significance.

In other words, you fell into what psychologists call a *secondary gain trap*. You were looking for A, but really hoping for B: looking for money or a promotion but really hoping for the reward of recognition.

Managing our minds is the gateway to wisdom, I believe. This isn't a process of assigning an autocrat to police your thoughts. Here's what it involves.

Go silent for a few minutes, as I did after my backyard workout. Simply close your eyes and allow your thoughts to enter your mind. Watch them, and when you see a belief, perhaps a generalization, pause to consider it.

The key question is: "What am I telling myself?"

That careerist in my example might reply: "I'm telling myself I need a raise!"

Fair enough, if this is a conclusion that has been reached using the Ben Franklin method. You make up two lists. Write down your income in one column, all of it. Do the same for your expenses. If your totals match, then perhaps you do need a raise.

Now your belief and your reality match, which is functional; you can work with this. Assuming you cannot cut your expenses, you will need more money.

But you should beware of jumping to the conclusion that it *must* come from your current employer. Could it come from another source?

Can you moonlight, finding a part-time or weekend gig to help make ends meet? Can you sell things at lawn sales, flea markets, or online? List all of the sources that just might help you out.

Of course, you'll also want to search for better jobs that can pay you more.

This example is provided for the purpose of saying that we should examine our beliefs and what we are telling ourselves before flying off to fix our problems. We may have defined the problem incorrectly, as I've said, thinking we need a raise when we need recognition.

And/or we may have defined the solution incorrectly or in a limited way. There is a wise saying that I commend for your consideration:

Don't ask people for what they are incapable of giving.

If your company is, objectively speaking, so unprofitable or poor or so far on the edge of extinction that it cannot pay you more, asking for a raise is senseless.

I consulted for a firm whose president spent too much of his day acting like a real-estate leasing agent. He was showing vacant offices to prospective subtenants.

That was a cue to me that I couldn't expect to be offering advice on a paid basis too much longer. If he couldn't pay the rent, he was in trouble, and he was at a point where he needed guidance well beyond what I offer.

There is an exercise that you can do that fits in neatly with what I've been describing. Keep a log of your beliefs, of what you are hearing your mind tell yourself about reality "out there."

If you're a job seeker, you might hear yourself saying, "There are no jobs out there!" or "I'll never find anything better than what I have now." These are obviously gross generalizations.

In every economy, including the worst, there are jobs that need to be done. Furthermore, in every economy there are people getting rich! Hard to believe, isn't it?

I'll tell you a secret. The people that get those jobs in tough times and that earn the fortunes are the ones that believe they can.

Even people who were down on their luck but won millions in the lottery believed they could!

So a major aspect of mind management is substituting expansive ideas for contractive ones. Where you are using impossibility thinking, change it into possibility thinking.

In other words, challenge your limited and negative beliefs with unlimited, positive ones.

"There are no jobs" becomes "There are plenty of jobs."

"I'll never do such-and-such" becomes "I'll definitely do such-and-such."

In deep space, it is posited that there are shortcuts travelers can use to get across vast distances instantly. Sometimes called "wormholes," these are visualized as tunnels or bridges.

Switching your negative thought to a positive one is like using a wormhole. It can work miracles.

In another section, I've mentioned the paranoia that fellow doctoral students shared that their key professors would prevent them from finishing their coursework and dissertations. Realizing this was a false belief, I chose deliberately to believe the opposite: that they would help me to graduate on time and actively assist me to secure a rare teaching job.

Thankfully, this is exactly what they did for me.

If I had seemed down in the mouth, and if I had acted like a loser, they might have been more tempted to kick me than to assist me.

Did changing my belief change my reality? Absolutely. Of course I had to work hard for what I wanted, but if I didn't tell myself the outcome was attainable, I wouldn't have summoned the gumption to do so.

Again, the first step, the inch-by-inch beginning of improvement, was in noticing what I was telling myself. It was in realizing that I was succumbing to the mass hysteria that was all around me.

I hope you'll realize and put to use the power you have to monitor and manage your thoughts. It is your spacecraft, one that can transport you to faster success and happiness beyond what you might have imagined.

If you'd like to learn more about this process, get a copy of my book and audiobook titled *Stinkin' Thinkin': 37 Mental Mistakes, False Beliefs, and Superstitions That Can Ruin Your Career and Your Life.*

7

The Power of Repeated Exposures

My brother had a term for certain watering holes where you were most likely to find amiable companionship, but not right away. He called them "exposure bars."

No, the customers didn't disrobe, nor did the servers. And there wasn't a nudie floor show.

My bro was describing local taverns that are frequented by regulars, by mostly neighborhood people. If you are a new face, no way are you going to get lucky on your first visit. You walked in alone, and you'll walk out alone.

Regulars wouldn't allow themselves or each other to become easy pickups. Social pressures, potential embarrassments, and worse, hooking up with the wrong person could be downright dangerous.

But as a newcomer, knowing this truth enables you to walk in, check out the clientele, have a leisurely repast, and then gracefully exit without incident.

"Where's the thrill in that?" you may be wondering.

The key here isn't that you are checking out the people. They are checking *you* out, and you're giving them the chance to do it in a low-risk way.

In another day or two, or on the following weekend, as part of your inch-by-inch strategy, you'll do pretty much the same thing. Walk in, sit down, order the same drink, look around a bit, but keep to yourself. And then promptly leave.

You might impart a quick smile upon someone that appeals to you on your way to the door. That's like leaving bread crumbs for birds. When your back is turned, they'll eat them up in the safety of your absence.

Upon the third visit, someone will start talking to you. They won't be able to resist. You're Mr. or Ms. Mysterious, and someone will be prodded to chat you up, if only to find out what you're about. At this point, you'll be on your way to almost complete acceptance.

It cost you three visits and three or maybe a few more drinks. But what did you gain? You gained credibility and acceptance, and you almost totally lowered the threat threshold of the other folks at the bar.

People that are on their guard are hyperalert to brash newcomers who seem edgy and impatient. If you are willing to invest four visits to a place, you're practically seen as a regular. You've shown the sort of detachment from but also commitment to the environment that whispers, "He's OK."

Speaking of watering holes, it's at moments like these that I'm fond of recalling Jane Goodall's excellent and pioneering work in studying baboon colonies. She did several things that I summarized above: (1) She went to a place where baboons hang out, to their territory. (2) She sat down peacefully, and kept to herself, mostly averting eye contact. (3) She left and came back again, and did the same routine. (4) One of the baboons approached her, but she didn't exhibit fright or flight. She accepted the individual coming into her space. (5) Finally, she was accepted and was able to make notes and study her subjects without incident. In a phrase, they got used to her, and she surmised that they accepted her as simply a peculiar-looking fellow baboon.

I've been known to descend upon new coffee shops to get out of the house and see new faces once in a while. Always the ritual is the same. There are strange looks from regulars who size me up. I drink my hazelnut brew, actually toting a grocery-bought quart of the spice with me. I make notes on my writing tablet, and I leave.

If I like the place and feel that it's conducive to relaxation and higher-level thinking, I'll return, do the same ritual, and leave. After three or four visits at the same approximate hour, I am accepted as a regular.

People will make room for me. They'll offer me a spare chair when the place is filled to the gills with thirsty humans. The milk of human kindness will flow as freely as the caffeinated brew.

In these episodes, we are transformed from unaccepted interlopers and potential threats to comfortable souls that others are relaxed with. What is the unwritten rule that makes this happen? As my brother said, it boils down to a matter of EXPOSURE.

You can prove the power of exposure to yourself. Simply join and observe what happens in social-media venues such as LinkedIn and Facebook, to name two. Certain people, maybe 5 percent of total posters, are responsible for 95 percent of all postings.

The first time I see their contributions, articles, likes, and miscellaneous sharings, I'm suspicious. "Who is this person?" I wonder. If they claim to be in one of my fields, I am especially inhospitable to their missives, thinking they're "poachers."

In reality, I have no greater claim to credibility than they have. Sure, I may have been posting longer, but what does that mean? Everybody walks into that barroom cold. We're all strangers, until we're not.

This is amazing, at least to me. There will come a day, possibly six months after these new posters have first arrived on the scene, when I'll begin to accept them. They could be, in my estimation, baboons, yet I'll impute to them a certain amount of credibility.

Objectively, nothing about them has changed for the positive. They have no additional academic credentials (which are hallmarks of knowledge, like them or not). They haven't devised a cure for the common cold or worse. They haven't built a huge commercial enterprise or started a massively helpful nonprofit organization.

They've simply paid their dues by coming to my attention many times during that six-month period. At that point, more or less, something happens in my mind. We can call it "brand awareness," and it signals that they are here to stay and I'm comfortable coexisting with them, even if they too are strange-looking baboons.

Propinquity is a term that has special significance in social science research. The iresearch website says:

> *Propinquity refers to the proximity or physical closeness of one person to another. The greater the degree of propinquity, the more likely that two people will be attracted to each other and become friends. Propinquity is usually thought of in terms of functional distance—that is, the likelihood of coming into contact with another person—rather than sheer physical distance.*

Here's what this means in practical terms. The more you are likely to bump into someone else, the more likely it is that you'll become friends, or even more. "The girl (or boy) next door" is more than a charming phrase from olden days. It signifies what happens in real life. If you see a lot of someone, you tend to bond.

They may not be your ideal mates, but perhaps they grow into that description by being ever-present. We even infer that our love or attraction was fated, a gift from the gods, when in fact it results more often from just plain running into each other a lot.

Hollywood movies are filled with what screenwriters call "meeting cute." Against all odds, two people bump into each other, or their cars meet unexpectedly in a parking lot. Or they simultaneously lay claim to the same taxi in Manhattan.

We've been saying, inch by inch, it's a cinch. But who knew this most important of all human endeavors, meeting, dating, and mating could be most significantly informed by physical inches of distance?

When Woody Allen joked that "80 percent of success is showing up," maybe he should have added that 80 percent of success is showing up and showing up again, and showing up again after that. Repeated exposures produce great results.

There is a famous tale told about the Shaolin Temple in China, home of kung fu and many martial-arts disciplines. One day an aspiring student arrived at the fortified door of the institution. Gruffly, he was told to go away. This scene repeated itself, day after day, month after month.

The monks wouldn't accept him. At last, desperate, the applicant came back again, offering his severed arm as proof of his sincerity. Only then was he admitted.

Extreme story, isn't it? But it resembles many legends about outsiders who aspire to become insiders. They keep showing up at the scene. Nothing will get rid of them.

It's like water. As a tiny droplet, it's extremely weak. But when it relentlessly presents itself, drop by drop, upon a rock, it will make that rock erode.

When I was flying frequently for my consulting practice, I sat next to all kinds of celebrities: comedians, actors, the U.S. Coast Guard's drug interdiction chief officer in Columbia, you name it.

I came to expect that I'd be seated next to these folks. They'd see me typing away on my laptop, and we'd start talking. Sometimes these conversations were simply amazing.

There is a famous actor that you'd recognize instantly. I had a really good chat with him. He was on his way to do a role that had him "riding horses and shooting guns in the Napa Valley," he boasted. Sounded cool to me.

We gossiped about some of the actresses he had worked with, who I agreed were especially fetching. The flight lasted fifty-five minutes, and perhaps forty-five of them were dedicated to our scuttlebutt.

Later that year, my football team was headed to the Rose Bowl. I belonged to a pricey booster's group that provided a lavish brunch before the game. As my wife and I took out seats, guess who was feasting next to me?

Yes, it was the same actor. At that point I felt I knew him. "Last time we talked on a plane," I recalled, "You were about to ride horses and shoot guns in the Napa Valley. How did that work out?"

It was great, he said, and we exchanged a few more pleasantries. I didn't run into him a third time, but if I did, I probably could have asked him to do me a favor, or vice versa.

Improbable as it is, this is how exposures work in real life.

Speaking of planes, there was a point where I flew back and forth to Houston for the better part of two years. Mostly, I took the same slights on the same carrier. Unbeknownst to me, the flight attendants knew me.

On one flight to Houston, I sat next to the CEO of that airline, who was very unpopular with the unions that represented flight attendants and pilots. We had a nice chat about business. I told him I was a consultant and mentioned the firm I worked for.

As I deplaned and walked through the vast airport, a phalanx of flight attendants rolled up to me with their luggage and breathlessly asked me, "How could you talk to that man! He's the devil!"

They were giving their boss the cold shoulder and expected me to do the same. On what authority could they believe I had a dog in their fight, as the expression puts it?

There is only one explanation. They felt they knew me and therefore they could call on me to support them in their cause. What told them as much?

Well, I had flown together a lot with them. He hadn't. So I was a natural ally, correct?

They had more exposure to me than to him. He and I seemed to get along. Maybe I would clue him in about how unpopular he was and he'd change or step down.

But I'm just this customer that kept showing up! Inch by inch, it's a cinch.

Decide where you need to do this, and you may find that it makes all the difference in summoning companionship—or something altogether different.

8

Inch By Inch It's a Cinch, and Yard by Yard, It's Hard

Federal Express is a great corporate success story, told and retold in case studies by business profs and by management authors.

In its early days, facing extinction by negative cash flow, chairman Fred Smith reportedly took half the money needed to cover the payroll and flew to Vegas.

Betting it all on blackjack, he won, and FedEx stayed in business to fly packages another day, according to legend.

That risky all-or-nothing play is the essence of a "yard by yard, it's hard" strategy for success.

It's like a Hail Mary pass. The quarterback or running back can unexpectedly hurl the ball into a crowd of defenders, praying that his teammate will leap at just the right moment and snare the toss for a touchdown. But the odds are stacked against its success.

It is far better to avoid putting yourself into a position where you need to bet the farm on a couple of cards or on a freakishly good outcome, no matter what the endeavor.

Yet this type of big-stakes gambling is the popular image of what plucky entrepreneurs do. Supposedly they take big risks and therefore reap big rewards.

They're the stick figures on the brink of starvation panning for gold in the scorching heat, and the Silicon Valley techies that live on packages of noodles until the venture capitalists fund them.

But this is an inaccurate portrait, according to my professor, management sage Peter F. Drucker. He said that entrepreneurs aren't wild-eyed risk takers. In fact, they are the opposite.

Most of the successful heads of new enterprises are actually risk-averse.

They're philosophy isn't "Bet big and win big." It's closer to "Bet small, win a little, reinvest it, win yet more, and keep going until you can afford to scale up your good fortune."

It isn't Superman's ability to leap tall buildings with a single bound. It's more like taking the stairs, a single, steady step at a time.

For instance, William used to record my audios for me. He had a small shedlike space in a business park dedicated to light manufacturing. Inside was a sound-proof and—I grit my teeth as I recall it—airtight studio.

That's where I recorded about five audio seminars. Every half hour, we'd need to crack the vault open to replenish the air inside the Soyuz-like, ultra-cramped recording module.

William didn't make much money with me, because I bought sixty to a hundred twenty of my programs at a time, for resale. He lived on soup and who knows what, wearing monkish sweaters that looked like frayed chain mail.

But then he had a breakthrough. Instead of recording and reproducing audios for authors like me, who bought a few sets and charged high prices for them, he encouraged people to record messages that they would give away, in bulk, by the tens of thousands.

Sure, his margins went down on each unit he produced, but because he was selling by the thousands instead of the dozens, he started to get ahead of the game and earn a good living.

William hung in, doing the basics, the blocking and tackling of his small business, long enough to have an epiphany that would transform his enterprise from a marginal survival mode into a healthy profit mode. His inch-by-inch progress paved the way to yard-by-yard gains.

William was smart. When he first tasted success, he didn't binge on it. He kept his expenses down, working out of that small, Spartan industrial space. He hired a helper or two. The only obvious difference was the sound of machine activity and the inventory of raw materials stacked from floor to ceiling.

Which reminds me of the famous billionaire investor Warren Buffett. This elderly Nebraskan is the founder of Berkshire Hathaway, a huge conglomerate with major investments in Coca-Cola, Gillette, Geico, and other companies.

Long after Buffett could afford to live in a lavish mansion, he continued to dwell in his modest suburban home, the one in which he has resided for decades. He is renowned for taking business dignitaries to lunch at McDonald's. He resisted the "earn big and spend bigger" temptation that many people succumb to, which leads to financial reversals.

Scaling up slowly, by inches, makes sense, whether you are earning or spending.

Savvy investors like Buffett often share a similar philosophy when they place their business bets: "Don't lose."

They still risk money on various ventures, but seldom do they risk everything they have, including their "seed corn," their main store of capital. Also, they diversify their risks, never putting all of their eggs into one basket.

So, if one egg breaks, the others usually stay intact.

When I teach negotiation seminars to career builders, I point out the importance of developing leverage. For example, the greatest form of leverage we can have is being able to walk away from a proposed deal.

This is called having a good BATNA, or Best Alternative to a Negotiated Agreement.

Let's say you're applying for jobs. What is the best BATNA to have?

It is to be currently in demand. This means (1) having a decent existing job where you tell prospective employers that you can remain, and (2) having multiple job offers to which you can go.

When you are currently employed, you come across to others as being highly desirable. See it this way: at least one other company likes you!

Between jobs, when you're unemployed, it seems nobody likes you. So why should the one you are asking for a job think any differently?

This sounds harsh and cruel, but it is the way things appear. How can you ensure that you won't fall into this trap?

Always be working! Never be completely unemployed, if you can help it. You may be hanging onto your existing gig by your fingernails—in other words, by inches—but you are still employed, and that constitutes negotiating leverage.

This sounds rosy, but how do you pull it off? Always be looking for work.

Keep an eye out for other opportunities. Speak to people about what they do, about opportunities that may be coming up at their firms. Let them know what your strengths are, and tell them you're always open to hearing about new possibilities to apply them.

These practices come up when I speak to people who are interested in learning how to ask for raises and promotions. Without fail, after I urge them to start asking at their next performance review, they wonder out loud, "What will happen if I'm turned down?"

I say the answer depends on your options, on your BATNA. If you have lined up other possibilities and especially one superior job offer, you can refer to it.

A company can puff all it wants about how its salaries are competitive and well researched and justified by the market. But those claims mean nothing if you can clearly and confidently state, "There is a company that thinks I'm worth more."

If your existing employer wants to keep you, it will meet or exceed that new offer. If not, at least you know where your next check will come from.

Speaking of getting paid, gaps in employment, as you probably know, are exceedingly costly. So it pays to make seamless transitions from one employer to the next.

Let's say you're out of work for a month while seeking another place to ply your skills. You won't see a paycheck probably for six to eight weeks. This gap equals roughly 15 percent or more of your annual earnings. How will you make ends meet during that lull?

More to the point, how will you earn that money back?

You'll need to come into your new employment at a pay rate of 115 percent of what you earned in your last job if you hope to recoup your idleness penalty in one year. If you get paid only 5 percent more, it will take three full years to earn back what you have lost.

You can see how costly job gaps can be. This means you need to time your departure from one place in such a way that you link up to the next place without experiencing significant down time.

As this math also points out, if you are going to suffer a long gap, this will cost you quite a bit. In light of this expense, it is important to ask, "Does it make any sense to leave my current employer?"

You might consider doing an inch-by-inch campaign where you slowly but steadily transition into a new job with improved pay. Keep your eyes peeled for job postings in different divisions.

Make friends with some human-resources people. Ask them what you need to do, and how you need to retool your education and training to qualify for bigger and better things. There may be a budget to support your expenses if you take courses part-time or on weekends.

Of course, getting a current employer to invest in transferrable skills that will be highly compensated elsewhere is a huge win for you. It proves you're ambitious and willing to take on more responsibility where you are currently working.

Plus, it puts your bosses on the clock, so to speak, with regard to using or losing your increased performance capabilities. They are smart enough to know that if they don't move you up the ladder, you'll carry that ladder to a different workplace.

With every course that you pass, get a certificate or a letter attesting to your achievement and have human resources place it into your personnel folder. This will keep your name in front of those that hire. They will see you as an up-and-coming employee. They may think of you first when they are given a new job order to fill.

Saving money is very hard to do, yard by yard. This is why payroll deductions are so popular. Every pay period, when a small amount is siphoned off to invest in a savings account or investment fund, it is relatively painless.

For one thing, that money never reaches our hands. Second, one big decision about participating in a savings program has already been made. This relieves you from having to decide over and over, paycheck to paycheck, whether to save and how much to save.

Most personal investment gurus advocate a "pay yourself first plan" that works this way, even if you work for yourself. The idea is to take up to 10 percent of your income or revenue and to set it aside before you pay for anything else.

By building this habit, not only do you build a serious nest egg, but you minimize the likelihood that you'll go off your program altogether.

Most of us realize that crash diets aren't long-term solutions to being overweight. What happens is that we deny ourselves certain foods in major amounts for a short period, possibly dropping some pounds. But we gain them back, and frequently get more rotund than we were before we undertook the radical, yard-by-yard reducing program. What we should be doing is an inch-by-inch campaign. Do just one thing, and do it consistently.

Portion control is a powerful tool. Put less on your plate. Or eat less of what is put there, deliberately saving some for leftovers.

Here is a similar approach. If you make a point of eating until you are just 80 percent full, as many do in certain Asian cultures, you will probably enjoy a steady reduction in overall body fat.

Overexercising is also problematic. If you like walking, don't force yourself to walk several miles right away. Literally, take baby steps.

When I drive to the market, I find a parking space about three hundred feet or more from the door. This forces me to get some exercise, and when combined with the cart pushing I do across the length and width of the store, along with carrying my bags to the car, this activity adds up.

But it doesn't feel like exercise, and I don't succumb to self-pity because I feel I'm sacrificing comfort or stuck hopelessly on a treadmill to nowhere.

Exercise, or lack of it, is an interesting habit. If you do just a little walking, you'll probably feel invigorated, renewed, and restored. Thus you'll be inclined to repeat that pattern or even to build on it with more exertion, with slightly longer walks.

If you sit on your butt or are otherwise idle, you'll probably start feeling fatigue. If you're like me, you'll be hyperaware of every ache and pain. And these sensations will bother you, and cause you to worry.

In a phrase, you'll feel hopelessly out of shape. With that in mind, day after day, you'll be very reluctant to start an exercise program. And you'll think that the amount of exertion it requires will be far beyond your capabilities.

The trick is to start on a super-small scale. Do the smallest imaginable amount of exercise.

What could that be?

As a starter, I like isometrics. This is the tensing and then relaxing of certain muscle groups.

It could be as easy as making two fists and holding your fingers in that position for five seconds. I'm going to do it now.

I can feel a tingling in my fingers and in my wrists. I'm going to do it again.

My muscles in my forearms have joined the process and are getting some exercise.

For my third set, I just added in my biceps, opening and closing my fists with each flexion. My breathing has been affected. I'm sure I'm pumping more blood.

One more time, still sitting down in my desk chair, I've just done twenty repetitions of each arm, and I've added deliberately deep breathing. I'm feeling pumped, as bodybuilders say.

In a few minutes, I'll walk into the backyard and do some vigorous karate exercises, combining sequences of body movements, blocks, hand strikes, and kicks.

While there is a difference of opinion on exercise and dietary programs that work, recent studies suggest that we need and benefit from much less exertion than we may have thought. Just doing practically any exercise for five minutes a day can have a beneficial effect on our overall health and conditioning.

Truly, when it comes to getting into shape, inch by inch is a cinch!

Sometimes the first inch isn't the fist you make or the arm you flex. It is the IDEA that you can and should do it, and that by doing something so modest you'll be making a big overall impact on your results.

It's very possible you are fostering some false or counterproductive beliefs about how good gains are made. You might be telling yourself something like this:

"If I start an exercise program, I'll look silly."

There is a mature lady in her eighties who just started ice skating at the rink we go to in Santa Barbara. She made her first appearance last Saturday, and like most beginners, she clutched the protective railing, using her hands for support.

Does she look foolish or silly? Of course she doesn't. She looks heroic to me!

As with most new things, they are hard before they are easy. We must permit ourselves to inch our way through an awkward phase. If we don't, most assuredly we won't make it to a graceful stage.

And there are eighty-year-olds on that very same ice who are exceedingly graceful. Two of them I know are instructors.

Balling your fists may feel awkward or aggressive, but it is one small way to start doing isometrics.

Another belief that can hold you back is that you need to be instantly successful in order to succeed. This is a trap I fall into, I must admit.

I am one of those lucky people: I succeed with most of the things I try doing.

There are many sales jobs that I have held in which the first contact I made I earned a sale. Indeed this has happened so often that I expect it and am slightly surprised and miffed if my initial presentation is rejected.

Sports have been pretty much the same way for me. The first time I lifted a bowling ball, I rolled a strike. Off the top of my head, I can't recall being 100 percent uncoordinated in any sport I've tried, although high jumping could be the exception. I broke my wrist the first time, when I leaped through the bar instead of over it.

With a legacy of instant achievement, it is difficult for me to stick with something that takes relentless inching along to succeed. I like making big yardage right away!

But I have had to alter this expectation in many contexts. One of them is academia, where I have accumulated five earned degrees, including four graduate degrees.

This simply cannot happen overnight. In some circumstances, such as in my PhD and law degree programs, I've had to work exceedingly hard and long to make what I felt to be minimal success.

Check your beliefs. Do they permit you to make incremental gains, or are they perfectionistic, compelling you to succeed right away? Adjust them accordingly.

Criticized for being a plodder, Abe Lincoln said, "I may move slowly, but I never go backwards."

That could be the incrementalist's credo. Make some progress toward a goal, however modest it may be.

Pause along the way, if you must. Catch your breath.

And by all means refuse to succumb to the common distraction that scientists call "social comparison," the trap commonly known as "keeping up with the Joneses."

Too often, we fail to measure our progress by what we've actually achieved. We don't look back and remark, "Look at how far I've come!"

Instead we compare ourselves to others, measuring ourselves against their achievements.

At one company I was selling business mentoring, and as I always do, I set my sights on being the top performer, the best producer, number one. Jimmy predated me on the job by two years. In fact, he was one of the company's first sellers; he'd been there from the beginning of the business.

I did very well, very fast, and I became the number two seller, behind Jimmy. I was the last person selling before Christmas break arrived. All of the other sellers had gone on vacation but me.

I made a few additional presentations, knowing I had a chance to qualify as top seller for December if I could only close one or two extra deals.

On my final call, I earned a double deal, which should have easily put me over the top.

When we returned in January, Jimmy was declared the top seller for December!

What happened? When I inquired, there was some lame excuse made about his having a deal that wasn't factored into the equation, but I smelled a rat.

What came out later in a thoughtless moment in a sales meeting told the rest of the story. The sales manager casually disclosed that "Jimmy gets twice as many leads as anyone else because he's so good."

What?

Of course you'll be top seller if you get twice the amount of raw material from which to fashion sales results.

The fix was in, and if it persisted, one way or another, I'd never make it to being number one.

Of course this made me mad. I left soon after realizing that cronyism was heavily influencing not only sales, but commissions, bonuses, and overall earnings in major ways.

Still, I did very well there financially. And looking back, I can see I fell into a trap. Sure, the system was corrupt. In a perfect world it would have been totally honest.

But I allowed myself to be influenced too much by how I perceived that Jimmy was doing instead of counting my own money.

As Peter Drucker said about this kind of circumstance, "We aren't so much motivated to reach certain goals as we are demotivated by seeing how others are rewarded differently than we are."

The emotion I felt when witnessing Jimmy's results was contempt. According to Aristotle, contempt is triggered when an inferior gets more than you get.

I was the better seller, but he made more money. I should have changed my belief so that I cared less about it than I did.

Sooner or later, even with the cooking of the books during contest periods and his getting twice as many leads, I would have risen to the top. That is, if I allowed things to inch along.

But expecting too much equity, and too much status for myself, I got in my own way.

Once more, we can see how inch-by-inch beliefs can work far better in achieving success and prosperity than yard-by-yard beliefs.

9

What's Standing in Your Way?

Up to this point we've been discussing how to adopt an inch-by-inch formula for success. We've mentioned some specific strategies, including finding an entry point in each endeavor, a place where we can begin, however modestly.

Until now we haven't talked about what is standing in our way. What keeps us from taking the small steps to success and achievement that seem so logical and easy?

There are ten culprits, and we'll go over them here. By the time we finish, you should be well positioned to sweep them away and get on with things.

1. **Heroics** get in the way. Frankly, doing anything in a minimalist fashion, especially in the United States, seems trivial. Where is the glory in starting modestly? Most of us have been brainwashed into thinking that our strides must be long and our day-to-day gains must be huge. If we watch or play golf, for instance, we celebrate the longest drives that miraculously deposit the

ball a foot or two from the cup. I'll admit this is a great achievement, but it is utterly rare. What we don't celebrate nearly as much is the putt, which can be inches or several feet from the cup. Putting looks trivial compared to those immense drives. But it is as much a part of the golf game as anything else. And you can fall way under par if you don't practice putting sufficiently and giving it due respect. By contrast, minimalism is respected in some other cultures, especially in Japan, where miniaturizing is an art and a science. Think bonsai trees and pioneering practical hybrid cars, which are two wonderful achievements of "thinking small" and seeking incremental gains.

2. **Impatience** is a huge obstacle. We want what we want and we want it NOW! One key characteristic of successful people is that they can postpone gratification. If something major is worth achieving, usually it takes time to make it happen. I mentioned that I earned several degrees, one of which is a PhD. This credential has enabled me to assert my expertise in many fields, and to gain a competitive advantage in sales, customer service, negotiation, and of course keynote speaking and seminar conducting. I shared the podium at a major convention with a colleague who was a fine motivational speaker, and seemed like a genuinely good guy. He went by the professional name "Doctor So-and-So." I never asked him where he earned his doctorate, because it wasn't relevant to our conversations. Then one of my clients asked me if I knew a good speaker who could join me as a presenter

at their company's annual meeting. Instantly, I thought of Doctor So-and-So. I phoned him, he was available, and he would perform for the budgeted fee. At that time I felt I owed a duty to my client to verify my colleague's credentials. What I discovered is he "graduated" from a paper mill, as it is known in academia. This is a buy-your-diploma factory that doesn't require much if any academic achievement. Calling himself "doctor" wasn't a true representation of his earned credentials. I informed my client, who decided to use the speaker anyway. He performed well, and everyone was happy. Afterwards, I suggested he do one of two things: (1) invest the time and effort to secure genuine credentials, or (2) drop the "doctor" from his professional title. I said, "You're so good at what you do that you don't need it." He didn't. He went on to author several best-selling books and to win substantial fame and fortune without using that title. Why did he bother with it at all? He couldn't postpone the gratification of being treated as an expert in some field. But that put him at risk of being publically unmasked as an academic fraud. But because he abandoned the title, this never came to pass.

3. **Focusing on the past** prevents us from moving forward. Where are your dominant thoughts right now? Are they in the here-and-now or in the there-and-then? It's all too easy to slip into regress instead of taking a small step toward progress. When I was a sales manager, I noticed an interesting phenomenon. When sellers made calls in a bullpen configuration, sitting side by side

in cubicles, some would finish an unsatisfying conversation, hang up, and then turn to their neighbor to revisit that chat in full. In other words, they failed to make a sale, they then dumped about the same amount of time as that ineffective call took, and they hijacked the attention of the person next door. Easily, the cost of that negative call was tripled in terms of the time it consumed. Usually the associate that was regaled with the dour tale would have one of his own that he felt duty-bound to recite. This entire sequence would turn a one-time loss into a five-time loss. We do something similar when we pass on bad news to anyone, including our family members. We experienced a loss, and that's bad enough. Then we restate it, taking someone else's listening time to hear it. Then they comment, yet another loss. And so this backward-looking sequence gobbles up more and more of our time and energy. I've discovered a way to plug up this black hole. If someone keeps saying negative things, at some point chime in and use a reversal. Make a positive statement, and then get them to agree. At Thanksgiving, one of my relatives was on a rant, when I retorted, "Yes, but we have a lot to be grateful for, don't we?" That stopped her in her tracks. She smiled, and the conversation brightened immediately. You can do the same thing for yourself. If you find you're ruminating over some past event that you can't seem to get over, remind yourself of something positive, some success that you're proud of. Then tell yourself, "And that's nice, isn't it?" Do this again and again until you cut the tether to the past and can move on by taking a small step forward.

4. **Waiting for the "perfect time"** to do something also gets in the way. One of my least favorite expressions is "Timing is everything." I've heard people say this in sports, in negotiations, and in many other contexts, and I can tell you, it is a gross oversimplification. Take the process of hitting in baseball. You can time your swing perfectly to meet the ball as it crosses the plate, but this is only one aspect of success. Your swing needs to be on the correct plane, and angled properly to address the spin of the orb. If you're putting a fastball swing on a curveball, you might easily chip the pitch into the foul lines. The greatest big-league ballplayers, like Ted Williams, have written books on the "science" of hitting. Timing is important, but by no means is it the only variable that governs success. When people ask for a raise, it makes sense to do it when the boss seems to be in a good mood. That's timing. But if you have no good reasons to support your request or you come across defensively or too aggressively, your pitch will be rejected anyway.

I've heard some people say, "There is no perfect time to do anything." I believe this is a better operating principle than waiting for the best time to arise on its own. Why? If we believe every point in time is somewhat flawed, we'll get on with what we need to do; we'll take action. There are people who see psychiatrists after they have made a bold move for the better in some aspect of their lives. Why do they see these professionals *after* they have moved forward? In many cases, they can't understand or explain to themselves why they waited so long to make a positive change! Some years ago, management guru Tom Peters wrote that *successful companies have a bias for action*. That phrase stuck with me, because it also applies to individuals. Branch Rickey was a legendary baseball player and baseball executive. He spoke about making the decision to trade a borderline ballplayer to another team. He concluded after long and hard experience that it is better to trade a player "a year too early than a year too late."

That notion encapsulates a bias for action. Waiting too long for ideal circumstances is the opposite, and it is a bad habit that we should avoid.

5. We assume that the **hard way is the right way**. I can't tell you how many times I've succumbed to the idea that the hard way is the best way, or the only way, to accomplish something. But my dad was fond of this adage: "There is an easy way and a hard way to do everything." As with so many of these ditties, teenage Gary had very little use for them at the time. But this notion has had a sleeper effect on me. It has grown in credibility, and I've come to see its practicality. I've mentioned that I earned a PhD. This was not an easy degree to obtain, I can tell you. Many of my fellow students were petrified about the possibility that their key professors would prevent them from earning this very significant credential. They told and retold horror stories about how former doctoral candidates that had passed all of their coursework were forced by dictatorial professors to toil endlessly, writing their dissertations, which were repeatedly rejected.

Hearing these daunting tales, many students failed to start writing these book-length projects.

I found myself getting caught up in this odd notion that doctoral advisors "eat their young." Feeling this paranoia grow, I took hold of myself. I challenged the premise that, like roach motels, PhD programs were relatively easy to enter but hellish to escape. I reversed the entire premise that my committee members would make it hard for me to graduate. "It is in their interest to support winners!" I told myself. How do I become a winner? "Be one of the first to find a job that requires a completed PhD," I counseled myself. That was a huge, but ultimately successful, inch-by-inch campaign by itself. But it worked. There was an "easy" way to complete my training, though many others insisted on taking the hard way.

At one point in that journey I asked one of my favorite professors, "When you studied for your doctorate, were you paranoid about whether you'd succeed?" He replied, "I figured if they didn't want me to move forward, they'd tell me at some point. Until then, I just did my work." In other words, he inched along, and ended up teaching at a top school that hatched a lot of great graduates, including yours truly! If there is an easy way, take it. Other people's destinies don't have to be yours.

6. We tell ourselves, **"There's not enough time**." Inching along seems to take a lot of time. If you think your days are limited, you can easily persuade yourself that you won't last long enough to achieve anything signifi-

cant. Therefore you won't take initial steps. One way we fall into this trap is by telling ourselves, "I'm too old." In some cases this could be true. If you're over thirty and you decide to take up gymnastics at an elite level, it's unlikely you'll earn a spot on the Olympic team. Still, you could become a serious senior competitor in amateur events. I heard about a world-class runner who didn't begin until he was in his seventies. Now in his nineties, he's incredibly accomplished, with several amateur world titles to his credit. Most of us have absolutely no idea of how much time we have left on this planet. My mother and grandmothers lived well into their eighties, but my male forbears didn't get that far. Whom will I take after? Or will I be the one to break all family records for longevity? I hope so!

A good way to avoid succumbing to the idea that it's too late or there's not enough time is to actively ignore, and when necessary, rebut the negative beliefs others foist on us. My sister once said something apt: "Have you ever noticed how we're always too young or too old for everything?" I'm at the point where, when I'm asked how old I am, I reply, "That's classified," with a smile on my face. End of discussion, because I realize folks are up to no good when they fixate on age. They are comparing themselves to me, competing, and that's never pertinent. It also ends up sowing dissatisfaction with where they are.

Recently, I read about people who live in certain longevity enclaves, in Italy for example. As a group, they age very well, often reaching a hundred years and more. Lots of reasons are given for their long and healthy lives. Diet and exercise and a lack of big-city stress are factors, but I have another one that I haven't seen anyone write about. I believe these folks *expect* to live long and healthy lives. They look around and see ancestors and friends making old bones, and why shouldn't they? Expect satisfactory completion of the projects you initiate. There's plenty of time, providing you get underway, right now!

All of these things can get in the way, but we can't let them!

10

Inches from the Finishing Line and You Turn Back—Why?

Much of this project has been about helping you to start. I mentioned in the beginning that we are fairly good finishers. It is starting that is daunting.

Still true, but there's more to the story. There are significant numbers of people who have a very tough time completing things.

In fact, they are inches from the finishing line when they pull up lame, or trip, or suddenly freeze right where they are. Maybe 99.999 percent of the task has been done. Victory is theirs for the taking. Yet they simply will not seize the prize.

This seems utterly irrational, but I have fallen victim to this problem myself. There are some nuances to it that are worth exploring.

When I was fourteen, I wanted to go to summer camp in the Colorado wilderness, next to the Dolores River. I watched intently as our PE coach showed the slides of happy campers horseback riding, swimming and fishing at the river, eating Sunday pancakes, shooting rifles, and having a rowdy good time.

"Wow!" I thought. "This is paradise, and I've just got to go." My best friend Alex, at whose house we were watching the show, was our finest athlete and an overall great guy. If he endorsed this camp, and it was obvious he did, it must be out of this world. So I reported back to my dad that this was the best thing since baseball and girls. (I had no idea how much I'd miss the latter.)

I wanted to go for the entire summer. My dad said he'd authorize two weeks, and we'd see how I liked it. I was my first time away at camp.

Plus it was out of state, about a thousand miles away, so Dad figured a toe in the water was wiser than jumping all in.

I told Mr. Crossman, my PE coach who did the slideshow, that I wanted to do the entire summer, but my dad would only agree to the shorter commitment to start.

Camp was pretty good. I got thrown about fifteen feet backwards by an ornery pinto named Leroy. Another horse stepped on my foot. Lucky I was wearing Chippewa boots with steel plates in the toes.

Shooting was fun and archery too. And we packed on horseback into the mountains for an overnight stay in a meadow under the stars. That was cool.

But the food was bland and I didn't like the regimentation. The worst thing was the fact I missed my girlfriend. I imagined her cavorting with the noncampers back at home, my rivals. She was very popular; beautiful in fact.

So I decided to pack it in after two weeks and hustle home. I'd had enough.

We were on a Native American reservation playing basketball on an incredibly beautiful court. My counselor told me to wait up after the rest of my mates started back to the vans we arrived in.

"So, you're going back home," he said with an ultra-serious stare. "That's a bad idea, Gary."

He went on to bawl me out for quitting camp. He said if I continued to quit things throughout my life I'd become a failure. Winners never quit, and quitters never win. His vitriol continued nonstop for what seemed like a full fifteen or twenty minutes.

His lecture was brutal. It made me weep, which was especially embarrassing, even if he was the only one that could see me. Though I was angry with what he said, how he said it, and where he said it, his message would have a profound effect on me.

I resolved to see things through once I started them. Almost without exception in the decades to come, I did exactly that. How else could I rack up five university degrees, most of which required sacrifices, a financial commitment, and rigorous study?

It was there on that basketball court that I became a finisher.

Years later I would understand there was more than a desire to impart adult advice motivating Mr. Crossman. In addition to being a counselor, he was a recruiter for the camp, and undoubtedly he had a financial stake in my being there for eight weeks instead of two. It probably meant four times more money if I stayed until the end.

Even so, finishing became obsessive for me, and looking back I can see where this habit has and has not served me. It would be decades later in a class with Peter Drucker that I would encounter a competing idea: *systematic abandonment.*

This is a recommended business practice. It urges managers to examine all of their company's units, products, and services and to "put them on trial for their lives."

Each one should be critiqued with these qualifying questions: Knowing what we know now, would we make this product again and support it financially? Would we reenter a certain business we're currently in? Is it profitable enough to justify our efforts now?

Whenever a "no" is the answer, that line of endeavor should be dropped. Attention and resources should be redirected.

At the risk of sounding flippant, systematic abandonment means we should quit early and quit often!

By *early*, I mean before we have flushed too many assets down the drain. And by *often* I mean that this abandonment technique should be repeated again and again.

Hearing this concept blew my mind. It repudiated the very idea of persistence, which is generally believed to be a significant virtue if not the ultimate one.

The difference is as stark as the one between an investment professional who says you should buy and hold a stock forever and a day trader who might sell a stock seconds after he has purchased it.

What about those people I mentioned earlier, the ones that snatch defeat from the jaws of victory? They're inches from completing something and then pull away. What's up with them, anyway?

One of their problems according to psychologists is that they FEAR SUCCESS. Success is theirs, and all they have to do is claim it. But they don't.

They fear the implications of success, what winning will make them do once they have achieved victory.

Late in his third year of law school, with only a few months remaining until graduation, my dad quit. His father was a controversial figure in the legal field, and as a consequence my dad got some heat from his professors.

Seeing how contentious other lawyers could be and how they denigrated his dad, my pop decided he didn't want to join the same club. The implications of succeeding were worse in his mind than stopping inches from finishing and potentially being regarded as a failure.

When I took up the mantle of law school, it was after I had earned three other degrees, including a doctorate. I resolved to finish the job, graduating early in fact, and then taking and passing the very challenging California bar examination on the first try.

But I already had another successful career as a management consultant and author, so I didn't really see myself practicing law, at least not right away.

I could succeed, going those extra steps, collecting my laurels, because for me so little was at stake.

Unlike with my dad, success didn't imply a commitment to a field and to colleagues I did not like or who did not like me.

Fear of success is often said by experts to really be *fear of future failure.* This is another reason otherwise capable people stop inches from the goal line. They believe, "If I succeed now, people will expect me to continue to succeed, which I'm sure I won't do. So it's better to fail now, when expectations of me are lower."

Somewhere lurking behind this idea is these people's perception that they're not good enough for the challenges ahead. In some cases, they feel they're imposters, merely posing as capable performers; sooner or later, the truth will be discovered about them, and they'll go down in flames. The shame at that point will be unbearable, so it is better to avoid that inevitable sorrow by accepting a nonresult or a smaller loss now.

Indeed, the closer they get to that finishing line, the greater pressure they feel to sabotage their success. This happened to some of the people I knew in the PhD program.

In two cases, these fellows saw themselves as sophisticates. They already knew a ton about a ton of things, so they didn't really need the ultimate academic degree. This was the stated rationale for mysteriously dropping out just before taking qualifying examinations.

Once you have taken your "quals," as they're called, you can move on to become a doctoral candidate per se. Then you write your dissertation, which is evaluated, and upon defending its academic rigor and quality, your committee of professors says you are Doctor So and So, or not.

It is a major showdown, like the gunfight at the OK Corral. You have to put up or shut up. If you don't have the right stuff, it will become known, and you will have exerted yourself through a brutal process for nothing.

So why not turn away inches from the quals? In this way you'll spare yourself later shame, save face, and free yourself to go into an easier field.

Again, it wasn't that these colleagues of mine couldn't pass their exams. They could, and that was the problem, because they feared success. More to the point, they feared that their success would be temporary, that they'd be unmasked as pretenders and imposters and any claims they had to intellectual superiority would be ridiculed.

Here's my opinion about finishing with mere inches to go. Even if you suddenly experience an epiphany and in your moment of clarity appreciate that you should become an X instead of a Y, if you are ultra-close to earning that X credential, then get it!

As philosopher Bertrand Russell said, "There is much pleasure to be gained from useless knowledge." I say the same about credentials. Snare the ones that are in reach.

I say this for a few reasons. For one thing, if you do complete the requirements, you'll free yourself from looking back remorsefully, knowing that you did not, which is a temptation with nonfinishers. Finishing can be seen as relief from future pain.

Second, you might actually use the credential at some point in your life. I have practiced law and still do. It isn't my main squeeze, but in a pinch I've been able to help out family and friends in their hours of need. And that has given me great pleasure, and them too!

The key question is, which tasks should I pull out all the stops to achieve? When do I need to persist? When should I inch forward to completion?

And when should I desist, letting go of what I've been doing up to that point?

There is no clear rule. Being a compulsive quitter, a ne'er-do-well, is not an option. Likewise, as I've pointed out, finishing everything may not be wise or even possible, especially when we are forgoing better opportunities.

Would I go back and choose not to do some or all of those five degrees? Sometimes I mention this achievement, and I'm met with rolled eyes, as if to say, "Why in the world would you need them?"

I reply, "Hey, I have a few degrees I'm not really using. Would you care to buy them?"

This isn't possible, and even if it were, I wouldn't sell them. Each one has led me to an interesting place and endowed me with greater insights and skills than I had before.

I'll leave this section with a story.

I had graduated from law school and I passed the bar exam, so I was a licensed attorney. I didn't make an announcement of this feat to my consulting clients, and it did not appear in my professional biography.

One of my clients irrationally breached a contract with me. It was just a dumb move that wasn't justified by my behavior, which was exemplary. I announced that they should continue with the arrangement we had agreed to because they were legally obligated, or, if they wished to be released from their duties, they could pay me in full.

It was then that I revealed I was also an attorney. In short order, they paid off the contract without hesitation.

The profit I made from that one settlement actually reimbursed me for every penny I had invested in my three-and-a-half-year private law school education.

So, if you have the choice, I urge you to finish, especially when there are merely a few inches ahead of you.

11

Starting versus Starting Over

Murray is an older guy, and for him finding a job is difficult. It isn't so much the fact that there's age discrimination. Lots of employers simply celebrate a youth culture and embrace the "new," which Murray is not.

He has kept up with changing technologies, and as far as his skills are concerned, he has not reached his use-by date. He has a lot to contribute. There's still gas in the tank, so to speak.

But his attitudes get in the way when he considers whether or not to start a new job. Recently he was invited to join a financial firm. The money wasn't so hot, but he could work from home. That would save him two hours a day in commuting time and a huge amount of wear and tear on his car.

But he didn't like how the new boss positioned his training. Murray was being treated like a beginner. He'd be given a script to use in his sales calls, and before he "went live," receiving inbound inquiries, he would need to role-play the script with management as a condition of being employed there.

He resented the whole idea of being micromanaged, even in this training phase of development. They knew he had industry experience, so why wouldn't they just let him go to work and eliminate the needless preliminaries?

There is an important distinction here, as he would point out to me. He wasn't against the idea of starting a new job. He knew there are always some jitters and concerns when we undertake a novel assignment.

What bothered him wasn't starting, but feeling he was starting over.

Here's the difference. Let's say you have been a machine operator for most of your working life. You see that you can become a clerk at a supermarket.

In that case, you'd be starting something new. That has a certain set of feelings attached to it. There's some concern you won't like it or fit in with other employees, but there's also a degree of excitement because it's not something you've done before. You've never worked a job where you interacted with customers, lots of them, every day.

But if you were a machine operator and you were asked to operate machines again, then you'd be starting over, feeling you're an expert disguised in a novice's clothing. You'd think, "I'm beyond that!" and "I know this task like the back of my hand."

In other words, you might approach the job, like Murray, with resentment, suspicion, and trepidation, especially if you were being paid a far lower wage than you had received before.

The inch-by-inch philosophy can help. It reminds us to cultivate a "beginner's mind."

In both cases, working as a machine operator again or as a clerk for the first time, you are at the beginning every day, though you may not recognize it. Each moment can be fresh and new, unless we dismiss it in advance, telling ourselves it is the same old stuff as before.

What it takes to get to this place of refreshment, as I'll call it, is humility. Artists must cultivate it constantly.

Take actors, especially those that are involved in long-running stage plays. Each night, five or six times a week, plus during matinees on Saturdays and Sundays, they need to perform the same script, pretty much exactly the way they performed it the previous time they did it.

It doesn't matter how much of a hit they were with their last audience; they need to climb the mountain again, starting at its base, the following day. Nothing is carried over. They may have some credibility because of good word-of-mouth advertising and favorable reviews, but they can't leave something out, a line or plot development, whenever they feel like it.

I've been in this position as a seminar provider. I have from time to time created "hits" that were well received by successive audiences. Some of my lines, and especially my jokes, were highly refined and polished. But if I didn't give my all to each performance, I would have let down those that attended on a given day.

Even if they evaluated the course highly, I would have known I was "off" here and there, and that would bother me.

Let's say I was on the road for a few weeks, and I was feeling a little under the weather. By the time my final seminar was scheduled, I'd be like a horse returning to the barn. I couldn't wait to hop into my rental car and go to the airport so I could decompress and recharge at home after being away and working so hard.

But I couldn't afford to phone in the program or cut it short. My high-school drama teacher, the renowned John Ingle, who achieved fame and, I presume, fortune starring in the daytime TV soap opera *General Hospital*, had a phrase for this sort of commitment.

He called it "performance discipline." It is the vow to achieve and sustain excellence in each and every performance, come what may.

Once I was doing a seminar in Braintree, Massachusetts. At that point I had been on the road for about three weeks. And my voice was shot from overuse.

I could feel laryngitis setting in the night before as I checked into my hotel. If you speak for a living, a rapidly deteriorating voice gives you a sinking feeling, and you start to obsess.

"Will I be able to get through my program? Will I even have a voice with which to begin?"

I prayed before I went to sleep. Testing my voice with whispers the next morning before the "show," I discovered the worst. I could barely speak at all!

I'll say this about my performance: it was the most animated I have ever done. I used hand gestures and mime to make many points. I never went through as many flip charts, because I wrote down several points that I would ordinarily talk my way through.

For inspiration and grit, I summoned to mind my training with Mr. Ingle, and that old adage echoed in my mind: "The show must go on!"

Amazingly, it did. My group gave me glowing scores on evaluation sheets. They appreciated what I was going through, and I believe they were even more actively involved with the subject matter and with each other than they would have ordinarily been.

I had to return to a beginner's mind to reconceptualize how to get through that performance while imparting sufficient information. While this is a dramatic example (no pun intended), it is emblematic of what we should do every day—without the state of emergency and impending doom, of course.

We have to remind ourselves of the adage "You never step into the same river twice."

Even if you're a machine operator doing your next machine job, it's new. It's not to be taken for granted. The fact that we can clean the slate every day in every way creates possibilities for inventing a ceaselessly marvelous life, no matter what we do for a living.

The inch-by-inch wisdom is in knowing that every day ushers in a new audience for all of us. They haven't seen our shows. And in a very real sense, there has never been an audience quite like them, nor will there ever be again.

We can label it as starting or as starting over, but it doesn't matter.

As long as we regard it as a fresh start.

12

Inching Your Way to Fame and Fortune

Artist Andy Warhol prophesied that each of us in our new age would experience "fifteen minutes of fame."

That's pretty easy to accomplish with today's social-networking technologies. However, it's a little more challenging to engineer fifteen minutes of fortune.

But that's exactly what I'm going to help you to do.

If you take to heart and put into practice the techniques I'm going to share with you now, you'll probably be able to retire a million dollars richer.

So please consider these to be your fifteen minutes of fortune.

How did I arrive at that million-bucks-richer claim? Well, if your career spans twenty or more years from now, which is easily conceivable, and you improve your negotiation skills only by 5 percent on the earning side and 5 percent on the spending side, you'll probably make and save about a million more than you otherwise would.

One of my participants at a UCLA seminar this year, a winemaker, whispered to me that he was going to take the tips I'm sharing here and earn an extra million within thirty days. No, I didn't get a commission on that, but, with a word or two of advice, I did help him to remove an impediment to adding a wing to a hotel he owned.

The first clear point I want to make is you get what you aim at. If your success aspiration level is low, that's what you'll get. Aim high, and you have a shot of achieving great things.

By now you might be a little weary of hearing about the 2016 World Champion Chicago Cubs. Disclosure: I'm a Chicagoan by birth, but I was mostly raised elsewhere.

When Cubs team president Theo Epstein and his manager, Joe Maddon, said without hesitation they were aiming at a World Series championship at the beginning of the season, I grinned. Bold idea for a 108-year loser, correct?

But that mighty goal became a marching order for the team. Anything less would be a disappointment.

In LA, about an hour away from me, local Dodgers management set the goal of being merely "competitive," which meant just making it to the postseason. I followed team news practically every day, and never did their president say that winning a world championship in 2016 was their goal.

Did the Dodgers get what they were after? Yes, they made it to the postseason, beat the Nationals, and then lost to—that's right—the team that would become world champs, the Cubs.

So, as I see it, the Dodgers' failure was one of LOW AIM. And most of us do this all the time. We don't set high enough goals, and that induces us to accept table scraps instead of being served a banquet.

I teach "Best Practices in Negotiation" at UCLA and at UC Berkeley. I'm going to pass along what I tell my classes at our first meeting.

If you set a higher goal of becoming a 5 percent better negotiator, you'll add a million bucks to your retirement kitty. Aim still higher, and you can become a world champion.

I was doing a consulting project in Houston for a company that packaged and sold government-guaranteed bonds to colleges, big banks, and retirement funds.

Typically they'd hire experienced sellers and pay them well when they brought in business.

If sellers didn't sell, they earned zero. They were on a straight commission plan that only paid for performance.

Not as bad as it sounds. Most new hires earned their first deals within thirty to ninety days, and then, with their pipelines filled with prospects, sales continued to roll in fairly consistently.

But one fellow, Joe, hired on and didn't get a sale in one month, two, or three. He didn't get a sale in his fourth, fifth, or sixth months. Or in his seventh, eighth, or ninth.

Imagine going home at night. Your mate asks, "How did you do?" "Uh, well, OK, I guess." "Did you sell anything?" "No, but I will!"

Anyway, it took Joe ten months to get his first deal. That equates to forty weeks of effort. At forty hours per week, that's about 1600 hours of labor.

All for nothing until he got that first deal.

How much did that deal pay him? ONE MILLION DOLLARS.

Was it worth the wait, the effort? Well, if it took him 1600 hours to accomplish, then he was actually earning not zero but $625 per hour for every hour he worked. Not bad.

Could you have put up with a whole bunch of nothing for ten months until your ship came in? The famous behavioral psychologist B.F. Skinner said it isn't how much we're rewarded that matters most; it's how often we're rewarded. The schedule is more motivating or de-motivating than the amount.

Joe's patience, his commitment, and his self-control were uncommon.

He made a certain deal with himself. This is where all negotiations begin, in our mind, with our aspiration levels.

Professionally speaking, he went deep-sea fishing, where the big catches are. His line was cast for a very long time, and then he reeled in exactly what he had been looking for and what he had envisioned.

You probably won't catch anything big if you are casting your line from the safety of the shore or from the shallows.

You may have heard this powerful poem by Jessie B. Rittenhouse.

My Wage

I bargained with Life for a penny,
And Life would pay no more,
However I begged at evening
When I counted my scanty store;

For Life is a just employer,
He gives you what you ask,
But once you have set the wages,
Why, you must bear the task.

I worked for a menial's hire,
Only to learn, dismayed,
That any wage I had asked of Life,
Life would have willingly paid.

You may be thinking, that's fine for salespeople and entrepreneurs, but how does that relate to me?

In every occupation there are some folks that are paid much more than others. You can be one of these people.

There are shoemakers and bootmakers that earn millions. Professors can earn fortunes.

Just look at those college professors of football, the Urban Meyers, Nick Sabans, and Jim Harbaughs, to name a few.

Speaking of professors, I was an underpaid tenure-track assistant professor at a leafy, Mr. Chips-ish midwestern university. A sweet school in the middle of nowhere.

I gazed out at my classes and thought, "Gee, these

folks are going to earn more than I do the second they graduate, and here I have three degrees and all of this knowledge." Worse, eight years earlier, before I had any degrees, I had earned at Time-Life Books twice what I was being paid as a professor.

I felt, and still feel, teachers should be among the highest-paid professionals in the world.

Here's what I did. I took that belief and the disgruntlement that came with it, and built a business concept around it.

I asked this perfect question, as I call it: "How can I do what I'm doing—how can I teach at universities—and make disproportionately more that I'm making now? How can I radically improve this impoverished college teaching deal?"

Tacitly, I had taken the first step. Inherent in my question was this assumption: It's POSSIBLE.

I looked around. I noticed that colleges of continuing education offered courses for businesspeople. These classes were often no more than a day or two in length.

I decided to sell my labor by the day instead of by the semester and teaching year.

I invented a course for businesses, offering it at California State University, Los Angeles during my winter break from my regular gig. All of seven people showed up, but they liked it.

When I got back to Indiana, I scheduled the course for Indiana State University in Terre Haute. They registered forty-four people for the class. ABC-TV news interviewed me at the scene.

We had a hit on our hands! I quit my tenure-track job and dedicated myself to being a day laborer. Within eighteen months, thirty-five universities offered my seminars, stretching from Hawaii to New York.

My income shot up by a factor of ten during those eighteen months. I was earning ten times what I was paid as an ordinary college professor. But still I was teaching, and I was connected to the university life.

Those classes led to my being discovered by the publisher Prentice-Hall. Over the next five years, we'd publish six books together, most of which became business best sellers.

Corporations invited me to speak at their meetings and to do extensive onsite training programs, and a business was built.

I still teach at UC Berkeley and UCLA, as I mentioned.

Changing my aspiration level changed my life. It can change yours too.

What's the next negotiation lesson I want to share? It comes out of this story.

There was this fellow in Texas who wanted more than anything to go to the Super Bowl. His beloved Dallas Cowboys were playing. But he was broke, and the game was sold out. Still, he said to his pals, "I'm going to that game, one way or another." The date of the game was rapidly approaching.

This fan noticed a small news item that said the president of the United States, a fellow Texan, was scheduled to undergo tests at the National Naval Medical Center in Bethesda, Maryland. "Well," he thought, "if he's laid up in the hospital, he's certainly not going to the game. Presidents always have tickets. Maybe he'll give me his!"

So he phoned the hospital and lucked into speaking with a member of the president's detail. He explained that he was a loyal constituent and asked, since the president couldn't make it to the big game, if he could have his ticket, please?

Well, legend has it that he received a crisp ticket in just enough time to see that game. And he had a great seat!

And the negotiation moral to this story is: HE ASKED FOR EXACTLY WHAT HE WANTED AND HE GOT IT.

It is well established in the research literature and in our everyday experiences that those that ask, get. And those that don't ask, don't get.

Women are about half as likely to ask for raises and promotions as men. They are underpaid relative to what men earn. Do you think there's a connection?

There's an old Zen saying, if you are bothered by the bumpiness of the road, you have a choice: pave the world or put on a pair of shoes.

But lots of men don't ask either, and they're underpaid too.

As I say in my audio program "How to Create Your Own High-Paying Job," there has been no reported increase in real, inflation-adjusted wages in the United States for more than thirty years.

You can blame that on corporations and on employers, and pave the world, or you can ask for a raise now.

If you look at the word, ASK, its letters contain all the authority you need to summon: Ask and you will receive. Seek and you shall find. Knock and it will be opened to you.

A-S-K.

Specifically, as a negotiator, set your aim higher. Ask for what you really want.

My wife and I were house-hunting, and we weren't completely satisfied. We were standing in the kitchen of one house that had an identical floor plan to that of a house we'd lived in before, so our feeling was, been there, done that. But my wife was kindly willing to accept it.

Appreciating that, I turned to her and asked, "What do you *really* want?"

She paused and drew a deep breath. "I want Alex's house."

Alex's house is a story in itself, the one that got away, six years before. Winding staircase, cathedral ceilings, plenty of light and space, gorgeous.

Hearing her real wish, I said, "Let's get out of here."

A day or two later, my wife noticed that Alex's house came on the market. We grabbed it. Happy ending.

Aim higher. Ask for what you really want.

If you are a seller, ask for more money than you're willing to accept. If you are a buyer, ask to pay less. This means, start high or start low, depending on your role.

Most folks blow it by asking for exactly what they are willing to settle for.

Let's say they've done a budget and they see they can squeak by on X thousand dollars per month. They'll enter a job negotiation and ask exactly for X thousand dollars.

Salaries are denominated in ranges. You should start 20 percent higher than what is merely acceptable to you. Through a process of give and take, offers and counteroffers, they may agree to only give you 10 percent more than that, or even 5 percent. But remember what I said about improving your deals by only 5 percent. It's worth a million bucks over a career.

That 5 percent advantage becomes compounded, because it is the baseline figure from which future raises and promotions and benefits such as retirement contributions will be based.

If you're thinking, "I'll get hired, show them my worth, and they'll pay me more at that point," good luck. If you start too low, you'll be tainted by it. You'll be seen as cheap labor, someone to be low-balled.

Paying you more will make them respect you more and dedicate more resources to your success. This is the expectancy effect, the halo effect. I urge salespeople to get the biggest salary, or the largest draw against commission, they can get because when they do, employers dedicate more leads to them to assure they'll get a payback on their investment in that person.

Remember this: in any career, it is easier to negotiate a better starting salary than it is to catch up later through raises.

What else should you know about asking? Ask again and again. One-time asking doesn't cut it.

Kids do this all the time, with great success.

"Can we go to Disneyland?" A few days later, this becomes: "When are we going to Disneyland?" This is followed by: "We're *never* going to Disneyland, are we? "

"I wouldn't say *never*."

"OK, then when?"

Gotcha!

I did this with my book agent very recently.

He said my publishers, the usual suspects, as I call them, wanted a pause in the action before considering more submissions.

I don't like these "Don't call us, we'll call you" pronouncements.

I let a week go by and then sent agent Dan a note. "Am I to understand they won't even *look* at submission if it's from me?"

He replied a few days later, more or less repeating what he originally stated.

A week after that, I sent another email. "Dan, no one can tell which titles are going to be big winners. I just got a serious royalty check that I didn't expect from my audio program 'Crystal Clear Communication: How to Explain Anything Clearly in Speech or Writing.' So even if I have a very promising idea, you're telling me they won't even read it?"

Another note back to me: that's right.

I decided I was going to pursue my project anyway, with different publishers, all with Dan's blessing. I spiffed up and expanded my proposal and sent it to two or three additional publishers.

I mentioned this to Dan in yet another email.

Waiting a few days, I sent him a note with the proposal attached. I said, "I know they aren't going to take a look at this proposal, but I just wanted you to have it in your files, for reference."

A few days later he wrote back and said he was submitting the proposal after all.

(See? He read it and liked it. I knew he couldn't resist!)

And then within forty-eight hours he sent me a contract for that project. Apparently one of my publishers liked it too.

You are reading that book, or listening to that audiobook NOW!

Ask, and ask again, and then ask some more. Take a tip from your kids. It works. (So does whining, but that's something else.)

Are there deals you shouldn't take? I've left a lot of money on the table, opting not to engage certain clients. You can learn all about these snafus from reading the last chapter of my book *Dr. Gary S. Goodman's 77 Best Practices In Negotiation*.

I can offer a few guidelines.

A tumultuous courtship is followed by a rockier marriage. If your contacts were a pain pre-deal, they may easily get worse post-deal.

Irascible people don't usually become cooperative.

And if a deal is joyless, or it turns sour, there is an emotional price to be paid.

As one of my clients in the mutual-fund business said, "Gary, life is too short to deal with unpleasant people."

There's some very interesting research on the persistence of bad feelings. If we feel we have been burned by a negotiation, or by a deal that has gone sideways, we aren't twice shy about entering the next one.

We're five times shy or more. It takes on average five pieces of good news to overcome the sting of one piece of bad news. (See the article in the March 23, 2012 *New York Times*: "Why People Remember Negative Events More Than Positive Ones.")

One researcher put it this way: "We hate losing $50 much more than we enjoy winning $50."

We're hard-wired to avoid negativity, to avoid what seems to be punishing. This is traceable to our survival instinct.

This explains why people DON'T ASK as often as they should. The pain of getting rejected is far more profound than the joy of acceptance of our offer or counteroffer.

We need to resist this reflex and ASK ANYWAY. We can even take a win from our losses.

I'm reminded of a scene in the movie *Raging Bull*, when boxer Jake LaMotta is counseled by his brother, who is also his manager.

"Take the fight," the brother urges, "because if you win, you win, and if you lose, you win." Jake was fighting a higher-ranked guy, so a good showing, even in a loss, would improve his professional stature. Plus there was a loser's purse—not the best payday, but still a payday.

Some deals look pretty dicey at the outset. Others seem too lean: where's the profit in them?

But sometimes they lead to something else.

Or they don't.

I was twenty-one and in the auto-leasing business in Beverly Hills. I was assigned the IHOP account, the pancake people.

Going back and forth with the CEO over a Lincoln lease, he told me if I gave him a good deal on that first car, I had a shot at getting ninety-nine more cars, the rest of the corporate fleet.

I wrote a very lean deal and submitted it to the president, who was tracking my progress.

He asked me, "What were you thinking?" seeing a trifling amount of profit in the paperwork.

I explained about the ninety-nine other cars I had a shot at getting.

"Let me teach you a lesson, Gary," the president said. "If the first deal is no good, you're certainly not going to make it up in volume. Every deal must stand on its own merits."

Bad deal times one is bad enough. Bad deal times a hundred? No way.

So there is a balance between short term and long term. If there is no short-term profit in a deal, beware. And if the long term is super-iffy, then you should pass.

Reminds me sometimes of Alice in Wonderland. "Jam yesterday and jam tomorrow, but when is there jam *today*?" Alice challenges.

Reasonable question, or, as my wife puts it, "And what's the *good* part?"

The Los Angeles Dodgers were sold to a group of investors a few years ago for $2 billion. The Guggenheim

Partners offer exceeded all other offers by a reported 25 percent.

They overpaid, correct? Not so fast. They saw a lot of hidden value, a big upside.

Shortly after purchasing the team, Guggenheim sold the broadcasting rights for a number of years to Time Warner for a reported $8 billion.

So if the Dodgers win, Guggenheim wins, and if they lose, Guggenheim wins. Meantime, the franchise's value continues to grow well beyond what that investment group paid.

And they haven't even developed the real estate that was bundled into the deal yet, the land surrounding Dodger Stadium.

Sometimes paying retail prices, or even bidding 25 percent more than retail, can pay off, provided that you know what you're doing.

It would be nice if the persons that negotiated that TV deal would also get involved in negotiating player contracts, but that's probably too much to ask.

A lot of our negotiations have nothing to do with money. Say we need to persuade a parent to take over managing a Little League team. Tread lightly there. I wrote a book, *101 Things Parents Should Know Before Volunteering to Coach Their Kids' Sports Teams*. One chapter is titled "Welcome to Your Second Full-Time Job!"

Here's a different example. In my negotiation seminars we discuss a case I call "Bonita Mar High School." Here's the scene. It's three weeks until graduation, and

Sasha's mom has been notified that the principal needs to see her right away.

The principal greets Mom and quickly gets to the point. The school's registrar has just informed the principal that Sasha has too many absences under state law to permit her to graduate with her class.

Mom is shocked to hear this. She had received no clue from Sasha that she was ditching classes, and the school hadn't notified her. Moreover, Sasha's grades have been all A's and B's.

Sasha did have attendance issues at her two prior high schools, and that was somewhat understandable. One was gang-infested, so much so that there was a permanent police substation located in the lobby of the school.

The next high school wasn't much of an improvement. With her parents' acrimonious divorce complicating matters, Sasha started raising herself.

Bonita Mar was to change all of that. It was safe, and known for its top graduation rate and the number of its students admitted to good colleges. Mom thought Sasha's attendance issues were over. This picture was supported by the good grades Sasha had earned, and Sasha beamed about her teachers.

The principal says there are two options: Sasha can be made to repeat the entire year, or she can go to summer school to make up the time.

Which is it going to be?

Do we have a negotiation here? Or is it an irrefutable proclamation?

We have a negotiation, don't we, because almost everything is negotiable. We need to start with this premise.

In a horror movie, I heard the nifty line that "Satan's greatest trick is convincing people he doesn't exist."

Likewise, savvy negotiators convince us that room for negotiation doesn't exist. They may even say, "This is not negotiable."

Horsefeathers. If you yield to this idea, you're done.

But why might we think this case isn't negotiable?

The principal has the aura of authority and official power that he can exercise. Plus, he says, state law requires Sasha to pay a price for her absences.

Do you agree, Mom or Dad? Do you identify with the principal? Or do you feel inclined to come to Sasha's defense?

Is there a justification for letting Sasha off the hook entirely? If so, what is it?

Should she graduate on time with everyone else?

Is Sasha merely a run-of-the-mill truant? Or is she simply a flawed or emotionally damaged honor student?

The key is to define what is most important in this situation. It is what I call *theme development*, and it needs to be done by the parent and by the principal.

As negotiators, you want to promote a theme, a definition of the situation that is most favorable or sympathetic to your viewpoint.

What is one potential theme?

What is best for Sasha?

The principal could argue that what is best is to teach

her a lesson about responsibility and self-control. She has a duty to attend. She breached that duty and must pay a price. Deeds and misdeeds have consequences.

Parents could see it differently. What's best for Sasha is refusing to stigmatize her with punishment. If she can't graduate with others, she'll be an outcast—the last thing she needs. And if she missed so much school, what is to say she'll even attend summer school? She might never go back to school or attend college.

What's another theme?

What is the overarching purpose of Bonita Mar?

It is to educate. The principal says students need to attend to get an education. The parent replies that clearly Sasha achieved, as measured by her grades and her satisfaction with her classes, without perfect attendance.

Or is the school's role to acculturate and to socialize students to obey certain norms? She'll have to make her way in the world, and, as Woody Allen said, 80 percent of success is showing up.

What other negotiation points can be scored here? Does the school have the moral authority to enforce the attendance codes if it has been derelict in properly notifying parents of infractions? Three weeks before graduation, Mom hears of this?

What if word gets out to parents or the school board, or to voters, that the school's attendance monitoring is so sloppy that kids can wander off at will to who knows where? Day after day and month after month before anyone catches on?

Aristotle said that rhetoric is the art of summoning all available means of persuasion. The same might be said of negotiation.

When money doesn't pertain to a negotiation, we need to get on the same page in other ways. We need to build bridges based on shared values, themes, goals, and by defining the best available choices, for all parties, at a given time.

In developing a new course recently, on "Negotiating without Money," I brainstormed a list of seventy-seven good, nonmonetary reasons that people should do what we want them to do. These reasons can apply to almost any situation.

This kind of thinking opens a parallel universe of possibilities to negotiators. All of a sudden, our overarching motivation isn't only profit or expediency, but things that are potentially more meaningful.

Here's how a parent could tap this reservoir of good reasons in appealing to the principal's greater mission:

What will Sasha remember you for, Mr. or Madam Principal? Were you the person that generously and graciously permitted her to graduate on time, with her classmates, feeling good about the high school in which she performed at her best? Will she take those good feelings and carry them with her as she enrolls in college in a timely way, after spending her summer earning money to help pay her expenses?

Or will she remember being broken-hearted that at the last minute she was denied her graduation, that she was punished for a pattern of behavior that was a carry-over from the awful schools she had attended before? Will she vow to never attend another school of any kind, and by doing so squander her gifts and bury her ability to make meaningful contributions?

Fairness is another possible theme. The parent could contend that making Sasha forfeit a timely graduation simply isn't fair to her. She is a victim of a broken home and multiple residences and schools in a short period of time, uprooted and relocated with no say in the matter. In light of her burdens, she has performed in an exemplary way. Especially without issuing any warnings, it is unfair of the school to enforce the attendance code this close to graduation.

The principal can counter that it is unfair to all of the other students to carve out an exception for Sasha. They should all be held to the same attendance requirements.

Another possible theme is "For every rule there is an exception." State law must provide an exception in unusual circumstances. (It does, our case says, for students who are often absent but have a legitimate medical excuse.)

My dad was a pretty good negotiator and quite an imaginative one. Having seen me act in high-school productions, he wanted me to get my fifteen minutes of fame. That's why he went to casting directors before he went to agents when he was trying to help me break into TV and movies, in a story I've already told you. It's also how he got me into his alma mater six months after I was supposed to apply—another story I've told. There is an exception to almost every rule. Emblazon this in your consciousness.

And there is a way to make almost any deal: this is crucial to appreciate.

Entering a negotiation, you should have two lists: a "give list" and a "get list."

On your give list are all of the things you can offer to the other party. On your get list are all of the things the other party can offer to you.

These, of course, can include money and money equivalents. Some things that are cheap or free to you can be of monumental value to the other party.

I was negotiating to do a training program for an international airline. I had experience with them, having done a successful program for a different department.

I submitted a proposal that called for a payment of $50,000 in cash, plus expenses and training materials. They could afford it.

However, my contact said his budget only contained half of the requested $50,000.

My reflex was to say, let's cut the program in half and go from there. And this is what the logic of best practices in negotiation urges.

When someone asks you to make a concession, get a concession in return. Don't make one-sided concessions.

Why? Because if they get you to drop your price once, they'll do it again, asking for even more until you cry out in pain.

In this case, Tom said he had half, so I said I'd give him half. If they take something off the table, like money, you take an equal or even greater amount of services off the table as well.

You can also use your give and get lists to offer and ask for concessions.

Let's go back to our questions. What can his company give me that can make up for the missing $25,000?

Airlines have empty seats that they need to fill. Tom could give me $25,000 worth of tickets or more, right?

No, he couldn't offer that, he said. (This guy drove a hard bargain!)

After establishing that I was traveling on business about 75 percent of the time and staying in hotels, he asked me this question.

"What if, instead of staying at Holiday Inns, you could stay at the Four Seasons for the same money? That would make your life a little easier, wouldn't it? Or what if you could save 50 percent or more on the rates you're paying now for hotels? That would add up to $25,000 or more in a single year, wouldn't it?"

I did some quick arithmetic. I was spending close to $4000 a month on hotels, so yes, I'd save $24,000 in the first year.

"And what if I said you could retain this privilege for many years, saving that kind of money year after year? Would that be attractive?"

He said all I had to do when booking my hotels was to ask for an airline discount, mentioning his airline and then showing my plastic ID card upon arrival. I'd get the discount again and again.

I could even use this benefit when I traveled for pleasure, pretty much everywhere in the world.

All I had to do was accept the $25,000 in cash and

do the full program I outlined in my proposal. I got a few other things on my wish list from him, and I agreed to his terms.

Today that ID card is a relic. The airline merged and took on another name, so I couldn't use the card anymore.

How long did it serve me in exactly the manner Tom outlined?

Our training program lasted ten months, but I used the card for ten years! It saved me, conservatively, $250,000 during that time.

It was worth ten times what I gave up in cash, and it cost Tom *nothing* extra. (Remember that question: how can I give the other party something that costs me little or nothing, but is very valuable to them?)

By itself a card was a card, worth maybe a dime, but with his special instructions it became a gateway to annual London vacations for weeks at a time in luxurious digs.

His give list told him he had a lot to offer to a consultant like me, and he made the most of it.

Our deal could very well not have happened. It could have easily deadlocked because of that $25,000 gap between what cash he said he had and what I had proposed and certainly felt my program was worth.

Notice I said in "what cash *he said he had.*" He said he only had $25,000 in his budget.

Was that a real number? Often what people say they have and what they really have are two different things.

Blaming "the limited budget" for a low-ball counteroffer, as Tom did, is a typical negotiation gambit.

How can you know if it is fact or fiction? You can't, unless you have a confederate inside the company.

Even so, there are lots of ways to deal with the budget issue. You can say, "Fine, I'll make it easy for you. Pay me $25K from this year's budget and $25K from next year's."

That's the equivalent of offering free financing.

You can ask, "What other department can chip in to support the program: Customer service? They must have a budget too."

I developed a catchy little comeback when people say they don't have a budget. "Typically," I say, "I'm an out-of-budget experience."

In other words, find the money, or let's involve an executive who's senior enough to write a check. Your people are worth it.

But Tom was especially creative, and he probed for ways he could add value instead of paying all cash.

This is called *interest-based negotiating*. He appealed to my interests as a consultant, one of which was saving on travel.

Positional negotiating is the opposite, and it is subject to deadlocking. "I need $50K," and Tom counters with "I only have $25K." We repeat this time and again, and the negotiation ends there.

Two kids are fighting over the last orange in the house. What does the wise parent do?

Cut the orange in half, like Solomon? That's typical, a quick compromise, but not optimal.

In this case, Mom went to Harvard, where they are high on interest-based negotiating.

She asks child number one: "And why do you want the orange?"

Seems like a dumb question, correct?

Child number one replies, "Because I'm really hungry, and please don't offer to cut it in half!" (Sharp kid!)

Child number two says, "That's OK. I need the entire peel because I'm baking a cake and it will flavor the crust. Half a peel won't do. I need all of it. You can keep the inside of the orange."

Ideal solution, better than a 50/50 compromise, the essence of a 100 percent win-win, isn't it?

Let's review this for a second. Each kid wants the entire orange, or so it seems. But the enlightened parent asked *why* they had staked out that position. What is the *reason* behind your position saying you need it all?

Instead of assuming the reason, we need to ask for it!

If we can get to people's reasons, we can find creative ways to satisfy their real wants and needs, not their stated wants and needs. And crucially, we reduce the likelihood of deadlocks and people storming away from deals, unnecessarily.

I said I needed $50K from Tom. He acknowledged that my program was worth $50K, but he showed me half of that money could come from a third party: hotels!

Getting a third party to pay for what you want or need is clever negotiating.

I did a $400,000 training program for a regional insurance company.

Later their CEO told me that most of my tab was paid for by a major insurance company that he did a lot of business with. That CEO tapped the carrier's marketing fund, one that is typically used for cooperative advertising, and asked that it be applied to my training.

Same goal, he argued, which was selling more of the carrier's coverage, simply a different means: using Gary instead.

These are some of the techniques that can give you that extra 5 percent of effectiveness, delivering a million or more dollars of value to you.

Good luck!

13

Embracing Personal Change

Sometimes I awaken in the middle of the night, not with any brilliant insight or marching order, but with sheer anxiety.

While asleep, my mind has been ruminating over an idea, or a problem of some sort that I can't solve.

I've come to take these episodes seriously, not as indications of deep problems, but as bold notifications that I need to innovate, I need to change my approach to some task, so I can break through to greater success.

One of these late-night episodes occurred when I was doing a consulting project in Houston, Texas. I felt frustrated that my advice, communicated in customized seminars, wasn't being implemented. I needed something else, an augmentation that would help people to turn on the ignition and boldly advance.

I got up, though it was two in the morning, and made myself a pot of coffee. After two or three cups, the bold idea came to me.

My trainees wouldn't implement my ideas until they were held accountable for them. I needed to: (1) fashion one-on-one training sessions to get them up to speed personally; (2) actually listen to them as they performed; and (3) formulate metrics, performance measures that I could apply to them, and that they'd be asked to apply as well.

For the remainder of the night I worked on these devices. The following day at the job site, I pitched them to senior management. They agreed my augmentations were worth a shot.

I refined them on the fly, and then started my implementations. To my great relief, they worked. I got the cooperation I needed, and my new techniques were put to the test and proven to succeed.

That formula that was hatched from pure anxiety, and probably a good dose of fear of failure. It went on to become a template that I would use for more than a decade. It would bring me large infusions of clients and cash, and would give me the confidence to disseminate my programs widely.

You've heard of "wake-up calls," sudden moments when you realize you need to do something, that you're missing the mark with your present trajectory.

I believe these wake-up calls announce themselves to me in sleepless nights or in fitful reposes. They may come to you in the shower, or when you're jogging. It doesn't matter.

Hear them ringing your inner phone, or prompting your internal alarm clock. They're positive signals.

Why is it that so many folks find it hard to adjust to change? For one thing, they live in a state of denial. They don't believe they need to make adjustments. They can just keep on keeping on in the ways they've always done things.

This may be true for a time. Yet as with the frog that is swimming in a pot with a flame beneath, what seems like a warm and cozy bath can turn suddenly and frightfully into a final resting place.

It has been said that insanity is doing something the same old way, over and again, but expecting a different result. If we expect to cope with changing times, we need to make our current routines obsolete before we realize that external pressures have made them so.

In other words, we need to commit to continuous improvement in the major areas of our lives. The best time to improve is exactly when we feel we don't have to.

This is when it is also easiest, when an inch-by-inch approach is possible and especially valuable.

For example, when I teach my negotiation seminars, I am always monitoring the effectiveness of certain case studies that I introduce. When I get bored teaching a particular case, it is a sign that I need to write a new one and test it.

Note that I don't wait until I receive complaints about the old case. I make it obsolete long before it seems dysfunctional to anyone else. If the new case isn't an instant hit, I'll construct yet another one and go through the same introduction process.

I'm not putting every case on trial for its life at the

same time. I'm making incremental changes, inch-by-inch changes.

Sometimes you know when you're stuck in a rut. Maybe there is this free-floating anxiety that you feel, as if a storm is brewing beyond the horizon. Although it's still out of view, you get the feeling you're a sitting duck, easy prey for something unsettling or cataclysmic.

This is a good time to change your personal routine. For me, this could signal a great time to find a used bookstore to haunt, or to visit the library and walk among the stacks.

I'm not there to find a specific idea, or a book that will scream, "Gary, here's exactly what you need to do right now!"

Instead I'll place myself into one of these unfamiliar contexts so that randomness can enter my life through these portals.

Another way of putting this is that I can get lucky by changing my personal routine. It's like adding new elements to a recipe and mixing them together: I might concoct something especially appealing.

Of course, I'm an author, so as I breeze along certain stacks of books, I'm being stimulated in ways that can help my career, just as landscape artists are nourished when they take scenic vacations.

Speaking of travel, altering your commute can change your routine and your life.

Author Joe Vitale was stuck in a dead-end job. At lunchtime one day, he decided one day on impulse to turn right at a crossroads instead of left. Two things happened.

He found an Italian restaurant that made great sandwiches. He had pined for just such a place, but had little hope that one existed where he was in Texas.

The owner would later sell Joe and his wife a home that he had lived in for many years, a place where Joe found great happiness.

There was also a street sign that he had never seen before. It read, "Quitman." Disliking his job, Joe took this to be a cosmic message: QUIT, MAN!

And he did just that, becoming a little while later a happy and successful author of books and audios.

This sounds like that catchy tune "Take the Long Way Home." What I'm recommending here is changing SOMETHING, perhaps anything, to see what happens, to see where it takes you.

After I studied martial arts for several years I used to tell myself this joke: "I *like* going down dark alleys at night!" The true part of the quip is that I found myself more comfortable than ever before in strange surroundings once I was convinced of my self-defense capabilities.

My discomfort zone became much smaller, and I found myself making conversation with strangers without the typical hesitation I'd had before.

As I've already pointed out, that martial-arts journey was many years in the making, but it started out with tiny steps. Many benefits accrued, even though I wasn't consciously thinking about achieving them.

Randomness is beneficial because it permits change to occur that we could never anticipate. Suddenly, taking that right turn in Texas instead of left, Joe Vitale changed his life and that of many others.

Speaking of Texas, I was on a speaking tour in the Amarillo area where the dean of a business school was my host. I spoke before a large meeting of an oil company and lectured on campus. Jerry, the dean, drove me to the airport.

Parked in the loading zone, we got into an interesting conversation, which, frankly, I was caught up in.

Time flew by, and Jerry kept asking, "What time is your flight?" to which I responded, "I still have time."

He said he'd walk with me to the gate. By the time we got there, after going through security, the plane to Lubbock, and to Texas Tech, the next campus on my tour, had already left the gate!

Jerry tracked down the gate agent, who explained that I'd missed my flight.

"No, no!" Jerry blurted out. "This is Dr. Gary Goodman, and he absolutely must get to Texas Tech today!"

I find this hard to believe, even though I lived it, so I can only imagine your face as I say this.

The gate agent got on the phone and repeated what Jerry told him, and a few minutes later, that plane retuned to the gate, and I boarded it.

Instead of being sneered at by my fellow passengers, I was applauded!

And my program at Texas Tech came off the next day without a hitch.

Extending my conversation with Jerry by just a few

minutes created an indelible story that I've told over and again. To me, it stands for many things.

One of them is that there is sometimes a "whole other" way of doing business in Texas, and Jerry pointed that out to me. It echoes what one briny U.S. general said in the 1800s: "One courageous man makes a majority."

It also reminds me of what baseball legend Yogi Berra said: "It ain't over till it's over."

Going that extra inch to insist that the plane be recalled to retrieve me saved my speaking tour. It also showed how powerful one person can be when a change in protocol is required.

14

Edison Knew Success
Is a Game of Inches

"Our greatest weakness is giving up too soon," said the great Thomas Edison.

He displayed world-class persistence. Ask different sources, and you'll hear that he failed to perfect the light bulb 10,000 times, or 6000 times. No one knows for sure, but we can safely say that lots and lots of times he came up short.

But finally he did succeed, and thereby changed the world for the better.

Countless benefits accrued to humanity through that invention and through the tandem development of electric companies, which carried currents to streetlamps and to homes and businesses so that the bulbs could be illuminated.

Edison is an exemplar of inching one's way to success.

From what I can see, most of us inch our way to failure. I call this process "little quitting."

I saw it in myself after I injured my toe in karate. I'm pretty sure I broke it, looking back on the episode.

And it wasn't in a sparring match or from helping to save someone on the street from marauding thugs.

I twisted my toe on the karate mat itself. My recovery was slow and painful. Finally I got back into the groove, attending classes and private lessons.

At one point, the *sensei* (master) challenged me:

"Why aren't you moving faster, going all out?"

"I'm pacing myself," I replied.

"Well, don't do that! Give it 100 percent!" he barked.

And prompted that way, I did, and I felt better about myself. And my toes ended up being no worse for it.

I was holding back, afraid I'd experience more pain. But by doing so, I actually slowed recovery from my injury while building up a mental block about surging forward in my karate career.

This was actually a form of little quitting. There is something to be said for the idea that if you aren't moving forward, even slightly, inch by inch, you're moving backwards.

As Abe Lincoln said, "I may go slowly, but I never go backwards."

There's much wisdom in this line. You may be in the same place, or you may feel stuck. The key is to do something, taking a small step toward your goal.

As I have already pointed out, I launched a very successful career by reaching out to universities. I asked them to partner with me in offering my workshops for businesspeople.

To do this, I called them.

This sounds simple enough, doesn't it? But it took

Herculean effort to lift that phone and to dial the number of Cal State Los Angeles, the first sponsor of my programs.

I was scared, and I was unprepared. I was also ashamed of myself because I had vast experience doing that ultra-simple thing, dialing a number and asking a stranger to buy something he or she had never thought about buying before.

In the sales world, this activity is known as *cold-calling*. I worked my way through college doing it for companies large and small. You'd be amazed at how many movie stars have done the same while launching their acting careers. Johnny Depp is just one of them.

By the way, Steve Jobs, the inventive genius behind Apple, got his start by cold-calling David Packard in Silicon Valley. He asked that honcho, who gave his name to Hewlett-Packard, for some spare parts.

Anyway, I supposedly knew what I was doing, and the fact that I couldn't instantly bring myself to do it, to apply that experience, felt shameful. I also felt hypocritical and inauthentic because the course I was about to pitch Cal State on running was on the topic of telephone effectiveness!

I was offering my services to teach a class to help folks to overcome phone fear, and yet I was petrified myself. At that point my phone felt like a 10,000-pound weight.

Why was I so reluctant to follow my own directions?

I had inched backwards without realizing it.

For the past two years I didn't need to sell over the phone to survive. I was teaching four courses at a different Cal State campus, as well as a class at the University of Southern California, where I was completing my doctorate.

You might say I was out of the habit of doing what I now knew I needed to do. Here's why that happened.

Inactivity is also a habit. It sneaks up on your slowly. Then it becomes the norm.

When I was working in sales, I had to act courageously. Call after call, I needed to summon the gumption to do the right thing the right way. I had to start at the bottom of the mountain with each and every prospect and then trek my way to the top to a "yes."

When I slipped, or when prospects threw stones at me, I had to regain my footing and carry on from there. If I didn't, my boss would scurry over and ask me why I wasn't doing what I needed to in order to succeed.

But having that two-year gap in activity permitted the vines of shyness to entangle me once more. I had to hack them away emotionally before I could contact that first university.

Fortunately, I did just that, and Cal State LA offered my program. We only had seven people show up, but they liked my material. This buoyed my spirits.

I contacted Indiana State University after that, and we attracted forty-four registrants, as well as live coverage on the local ABC-TV news outlet. Within eighteen months, my seminars we offered by thirty-five universities from Hawaii to New York.

Now here's what's interesting. I was invited to speak at numerous companies about telephone selling. My programs were well attended, and folks really appreciated the techniques I gave them.

Every now and then people would ask me: "How good are YOU on the phone?"

Of course, I thought I was good. After all, someone at their firm came to my public seminar and liked what he heard. And I knew things my trainees didn't know.

But as I was succeeding, I was selling less because I didn't have to sell. So my own phone fear returned, inch by inch, creeping up on me.

My worst fear was that my trainees would say, "YOU do it! Show us what YOU can do!"

I've just read about LA Dodgers pitcher Brandon Mc-Carthy. He told *The Los Angeles Times* that at one point over the past few years he'd caught a case of the "yips."

It's not a physical condition, but a mental one. Suddenly you can't throw a ball with accuracy in the intended direction.

It is a scary phenomenon. At some level you lose confidence in a move that practically every high-school ballplayer can do.

I was starting to get the yips when it came to using the phone to demonstrate phone skills.

Finally I conquered the problem by signing up on the sly to sell at a few different companies that weren't my clients.

I rose to the top quickly and proved once more that I could make rain as well as train.

But those first phone calls were tough. They quickly became easy again as I inched my way back into practice.

15

Inching Your Way to Happiness

Finding himself in a funk, philosopher Eckhart Tolle discovered wisdom in the following inch-by-inch concept: "Any action is often better than no action."

In other words, do something, anything, that isn't part of your regular routine. This can become a new portal to happiness.

This statement is redolent with implications.

Let's look more deeply into it. "Any action is often better than no action." Note that Tolle isn't saying action is *always* better. "*Often* better" is his phrasing.

Just so you know, there are people that believe doing nothing is "sometimes the highest form of action." California's two-time governor Jerry Brown made that comment decades ago.

To return to Tolle, he goes on to add, "Especially if you've been stuck." We all know that feeling of entropy. We could be stuck in what feels like a deathly dull routine. We greet the same job, same classes, same faces, and the same places, day after day. We're rusting away like an abandoned car in a field. We don't feel that we're making progress toward a meaningful goal.

In this case, doing something random, taking the "any" action Tolle is speaking of, makes sense, because it will alter the status quo. I walk into unfamiliar libraries and bookstores, patrolling the stacks for interesting titles.

It's free, and typically browsers are welcomed. Finding new places to have coffee while I write my stream-of-consciousness notes is also very cool.

I've found that my "twenty minutes of brilliance" are likely to come in unusual settings. Creativity thrives in novel situations.

I hear people using clichés that suddenly sound like great book titles and articles, possibly with the slightest alteration.

Our brains are hard-wired to respond to novelty. We actually crave it, and if our stimuli don't change every now and then, and especially if we feel we have no influence or power over them, we space out, go to sleep, or rebel.

I've mentioned at least obliquely that we can "script" success. Salespeople and customer-service folks use scripts for economy and effectiveness.

But they can get dull. So empowering people to make slight subtractions, additions, and alterations is essential in order to make sure they remain interested and successful.

If we're too lax, and they are permitted to make it all up as they go along, very quickly they'll shoot themselves in the wallet, experiencing plummeting effectiveness.

Perfect compliance with a script doesn't work either, because no matter how effective a patterned conversation is, users will defeat it if they cannot personalize it somehow.

"Not too loose and not too tight" seems to be the right prescription for people to get up to speed and to sustain success. Yet we need to heed what Tolle is saying.

When we're stuck in a rut, we need to power out of it by making a change—any change.

He says this is required "especially if you have been stuck in an unhappy situation." I want to focus for a minute on the last two words in this phrase: "unhappy situation."

Note that he doesn't say, "*if* you're unhappy," as if happiness and its seeming opposite are long-term, fixed states of being.

Happiness is contextually based. We're in unhappy situations more than we can be said to "be unhappy." There are three things we can do to make a positive change: (1) leave the situation; (2) change the situation; or (3) accept the situation.

All three options are actions. The last one, accepting the situation, isn't the same as remaining stuck. To an outsider, we might seem to be in the same place as we were yesterday. It appears that we haven't even moved an inch.

Not so, because our attitude about where we are has shifted. This is actually a huge alteration, especially if we have been fighting where we are or downing ourselves because of it.

I developed a bone spur in my foot several months ago. It was painful, and after doing some research I determined that I could either have surgery or let it heal by itself.

Jogging and even walking around the block were suddenly out of the question. I like being active, so this was very disappointing.

I especially missed doing what are called "all basics" in karate. This looks like a powerful and violent dance routine, and it enables me to use different combinations of hand strikes, kicks, blocks, and parries, all while I am striding forward and to the rear.

The idea of doing my all basics at this point seemed, frankly, impossible. But I remembered some of my training. I learned how to control pain by pushing it out of my body.

I decided my pain probably couldn't get worse, so I did a very mild form of all basics. I permitted myself to go back and forth just once in my yard .

Amazingly, I didn't writhe in pain. I was OK. Indeed, I was better than OK. I felt energized, and my foot pain, while still present, was overwhelmed by my joy at taking control again of my physicality.

My basics routine expanded and became more concussive, without worsening my situation. I air-kicked in all directions, and I moved to and fro. It was actually an invigorating victory for me.

I was getting back into an exercise routine that I like, all because I accepted my foot pain. Sure, I started to actively push it out, and that helped too. But the key was telling myself, "Look, if you're going to be in pain anyway, why not get into shape?"

We're saying that happiness is a situation, not a form of being, unless we make it so. Of course, the same applies to unhappiness.

"I am an unhappy person" is really a dumb thing to say to oneself because it implies this status is *permanent*, *personal*, and *pervasive*.

According to psychologist and author Dr. Martin Seligman, it is these "three P's" that cause us to feel unhappy and even depressed. If you want to get stuck and stay stuck, tell yourself that what happens to you is personal, it is pervasive, and it is permanent.

Alternatively, we could say, "I am choosing to not find sufficient joy in what I'm doing, and I need to look more creatively at my circumstances and deliberately emphasize the positive."

What if I had been wrong about doing all basics, and my pain worsened? What if I had caused an even greater injury to myself?

Well, Tolle's passage says I would have learned something! Maybe that this isn't the sort of disability that you want to inflame. Perhaps it was bravado over brains that led me to take such a stupid course of action, and I'll vow to be smarter next time.

But by doing it "my way," I did learn some good things. My intuition and training are pretty good. I can fight through pain, as I've been taught to do. My karate moves are still a force of nature that one may behold, if only in my own backyard.

The old routine of accepting the pain without the gain had lost its appeal. I chose to get some benefit from my injury instead.

We know this as turning lemons into lemonade, a good practice that's ages old. Now I'll have entire days where I "forget" I'm in pain.

There's a Carly Simon song that says, "I haven't got time for the pain." I can honestly say I understand what she's singing about!

Let me point out this isn't about masochism, finding pleasure *in* pain. It is finding pleasure in what would be an otherwise predominantly painful situation.

Finally, Tolle points out, "If you remain stuck, you learn nothing." This is one of the greatest indictments against inactivity, as I see it.

As I point out in my book *Dr. Gary S. Goodman's 77 Best Practices In Negotiation*, the deals I regret the most are the ones I did *not* do. At least five prominent opportunities come to mind.

In one case I declined to ink an agreement that came to me out of the blue. A division of CBS asked me to record a video that it would produce, edit, and sell. I was offered a serious advance against royalties. My attorney found something he didn't like in the contract, and I accepted his bad advice.

What if that agreement had ushered in some troubles of the type he envisioned? Weighing the merits of going forward against the downside risks, I can clearly see that the worst-case scenario was unlikely to occur.

And what if it did? I could handle it, finding—that's right—the upside to the downside.

As boxer Jake LaMotta's brother said: "Take the fight, because if you win, you win. And if you lose, you win!" The only way LaMotta could lose would be by avoiding the fight, by staying stuck where he was, as Tolle would describe it.

So doing SOMETHING, anything—even a random thing or an uncomfortable thing or a new thing—all of these moves work.

They help you to inch your way to happiness.

16

Bruce Lee's One-Inch Punch

Bruce Lee is one of the most revered martial-arts actors of all time. He laid the cinematic groundwork for Chuck Norris, Jet Li, and a huge number of stars in that action genre from around the world.

While some of his scenes were flashy and minutely choreographed, building on his form as a one-time cha-cha dancing champion, I remember Lee also for his contributions to the martial art he created in both words and moves. He called it Jeet Kune Do.

The centerpiece of this discipline is based on the idea of leverage. The following question frames the essential pursuit:

How can we get the most power and effectiveness from the least amount of effort?

Specifically, how can we use our bodies, which can be slight and weak (and which his was, inherently), and quietly transform them into spectacular fighting platforms, like a battleship?

He found power in the idea of the microcosm, the

smallest unit of effort that he could summon. Just as splitting the atom unleashed huge destructive power, Lee focused on what he called:

THE ONE-INCH PUNCH.

Of course this device, which I'll explain in a minute, was a showcase for the theme we have been discussing throughout this book: the game is one of inches, and winners make the most of them.

Bruce Lee and Mr. Miyagi in the movie *The Karate Kid* shared a common agreement about power. Miyagi counseled young Daniel that "there is no TRY in karate."

Meaning, if you are "efforting" your strikes and kicks and parries, you are going to be too tense and will actually diminish your speed and impact. Trying to be fast, or to hit hard, slows you down.

One set of muscles, which thinks it is assisting the striking set of muscles, actually slows them down.

I happen to believe that this self-defeating dynamic is emblematic of any kind of purpose-driven achievement. If we focus too much on obtaining an end result, and we stress ourselves over reaching it, we make that target so elusive that it evades us.

This translates to the following instruction for physical speed and power: Be like a loose whip while in the early stages of executing a move. Then speed up and SNAP with an explosion at the end.

Lee's one-inch punch embodied this principle. By placing his relaxed fist only an inch away from a man's chest and then thrusting, Lee could topple his target and do extraordinary harm, if he chose to.

Scholars have studied the physics of this move. They concluded that at the time of impact, Lee's entire body was marshaled into the action, adding energy to his crushing blow.

When you are in the martial arts, as I have been for many years, you read and hear a lot about the concept of chi energy. This is what acupuncturists are stimulating with their needles and what acupressurists are arousing with their fingers.

Hundred-year-old tai chi practitioners are seen in parks from San Francisco's Golden Gate to Beijing using the graceful, slow-motion moves. They regularly channel chi in a flowing form of spiritual propulsion.

We should apply the wisdom of chi and the one-inch punch broadly, in many contexts. By doing small things mindfully, we can unleash amazing impacts.

I recall being a frustrated young college professor who didn't want to experience "Groundhog Day," as depicted in the movie bearing this title. I cringed at the idea of repeating the routine I was in for the following thirty years.

A month before, I had developed a short course for grown-ups that I delivered only once at Cal State Los Angeles. It was a minor success that I decided to build on by expanding the number of schools offering the class.

When I returned to Indiana after teaching the LA class, I resolved to call a director of continuing education at another university, situated about forty miles away.

I was so nervous! I felt so much was riding on this conversation. So I decided to "script it," putting down on paper what I was going to say to get the director to agree to sponsor a class given by me, a stranger.

At first, I could see my words were sounding stilted, too stuffy and formal, and the text was way too long. It was also too manipulative, and I sensed the listener would hear my gears gnashing in the background.

I pared away sentence after sentence until all that was left was a brief self-introduction, saying I taught nearby and I was wondering what might be involved in bringing my new course to his campus.

The entire talk lasted twenty seconds, if that. Then it was his turn to respond.

Miraculously, he must have liked both what he heard and my direct approach. He asked if I had done it before, which I had. He then asked if I could send him a course description and I did, and we were off to the races.

The class was a hit, very well attended and highly evaluated. I was invited back to that campus again and again.

What did I do? Well, it was so simple, so compact, my twenty-second chat, that I felt confident I could repeat it to other directors far and wide. This is exactly what I did with astonishing success.

In record time, less than eighteen months, my class was conducted at 35 colleges from Hawaii to New York. That class led to a spinoff, and eventually to the six titles a year I wrote for Prentice-Hall, making me a best-selling business-book author.

Books brought me prestige as well as invitations from around the world to speak and to do corporate trainings.

My one-inch punch, that twenty-second pitch, split the atom for me, creating fission that catalyzed a chain reaction lasting decades, bringing me fun and treasure and a very full life.

Inch by inch, it's a cinch. Bruce Lee knew, and now you do too!

17

Inch Your Way Back to Financial Recovery

As I write these words in early 2017, we have a new president of the United States.

After a long and acrimonious campaign, he has become the most powerful individual in the world.

Reputed to be one of the world's billionaires, he is also a person that has taken his companies into bankruptcy. Which raised this question on the campaign trail: is he a savvy businessperson or a failed one?

In truth, the answer is, both.

While bankruptcy is an extreme measure to take to reduce or eliminate debt, it is also sanctioned in the United States Constitution. It is a right that citizens of the country may exercise, as he has done.

In England, and elsewhere, people who couldn't pay their bills were frequently sent to debtor's prisons. They faced criminal consequences for spending beyond their means and for failing to succeed in business.

This punishment came to be regarded as counterproductive and brutal.

There is still a social stigma attached to financial "failure," as it is sometimes considered. But if there is no recovery from failure, fewer people will take the sorts of risks that enable them to create wealth for themselves and others.

Getting capital, loans, and investments is often a necessary part of starting and doing business. Without extensions of credit, people can't buy their homes or cars until they have accumulated the entire purchase price, which is an unrealistic expectation.

And without widespread credit, the economy shrinks, throwing people out of work.

So what we know is this: Credit will exist. Some people will use it well and wisely, living within their means. Others will not, whether they are at fault or not. They may fall suddenly ill or have to care for a loved one, or are unexpectedly jobless and without sufficient income to cover their obligations.

But there are various ways of recovering if you find yourself behind in your bills, and this section will point to a few. One of them is through *formal debt resolution*. You can appoint a company or a nonprofit organization to negotiate a repayment plan that will retire your obligations over a period of years.

Consumer credit-counseling agencies exist for this purpose. They require you to assemble your unpaid bills and to create a budget that can help you to pay them off. Typically, creditors agree to freeze or to reduce interest rates on the accounts that you retire in this manner.

You are also discouraged from taking on any additional debt while you are reducing your existing ones. Any outstanding and untapped credit cards are surrendered.

Many of these counseling agencies are funded by creditors, so their bias is to help creditors to receive as much of a payback from you as is reasonably possible. Still, they help the consumer by serving as intermediaries and by helping to structure the debt-payback program.

One reason people appreciate these agencies is that they impose discipline and restore order to what might have become a chaotic pattern of overspending.

There are commercial companies that can also arrange debt settlement. If you are in arrears on your bills, you may have received a direct-mail solicitation from these firms.

Unlike nonprofit credit-counseling agencies, debt reducers are in business to do just that—to reduce the amount you owe. They contact credit-card companies on your behalf, along with health-care providers, and actively negotiate a resolution of your bills.

Some of these firms claim that they can reduce your payback obligation to mere "pennies on the dollar," but this is unrealistic. They may be able to reduce debts from 25 to 50 percent of their existing levels, but this is only part of the story.

How do they get paid for their expertise? They usually charge a percentage of what they save you.

For instance, let's say you owe $10,000 to a basketful of creditors. They'll contact each one and talk them into accepting less. Let's say the average creditor agrees to halve your bill, so you end up owing $5000, which is a large discount.

The debt reducer will charge 30 percent of $5000 saved, which is $1500. So your total payback will be $6500 out of that original figure of $10,000. Your net savings is 35 percent of your debt.

Every firm is different, so how much they charge will vary. By law, they are forbidden from charging you an up-front fee for their services. They receive their 30 percent of your savings each month that you pay back the reduced debt. If your payment is $300, then $90 of that payment is going to them.

Another way of stating this is to say the debt-settlement company earns nothing until they negotiate with all of your participating creditors and successfully reduce your debts with them. Only then do you make your payments. So in a very real sense, they are going out on a limb for you, putting out substantial effort over time to arrange your payback program, without seeing any cash flow from those efforts.

If you suddenly pull out of your program or stop making payments or experience further setbacks that make your payments partial or sporadic, the debt settlers see their income from your account drop, or stop altogether.

Above I mentioned that these intermediaries deal with *participating* creditors. Not all creditors will do business with debt-settlement companies.

For example, some credit unions refuse to participate. What impact does this have on your program?

It leaves you on your own to fashion a program with

these creditors that will meet your needs. In most cases, creditors will have some alternative payment plans they can offer you, if only as a short-term expedient to help you as you regain your financial footing.

At this point, you might be wondering, "Can I simply cut out the intermediary, the debt-resolution company, and negotiate directly with my own creditors?"

You can. But those commercial debt settlers will tell you they can negotiate much more effectively for you than you can on your own. There's some truth in this claim.

Think about it for a minute. In many cases debt settlers have long-term relationships with your creditors. This gives them a database of transactions they can look to to indicate how much of a discount they can expect to get from each one.

Let's say you owe creditor A $5000. The debt settler has been successful knocking that down to half, to $2500. Your creditor might exhaust you with a campaign of robotic voice mails and personal calls and ceaseless emails.

Multiply their calls by the number of creditors you owe, and you're being deluged with these annoying and distracting contacts.

Like a tough piece of meat that has been marinated, you're falling apart; you're super-tender, emotionally. You are in no condition to negotiate dispassionately, as professionals can do for you. Plus, as I mentioned, you don't know how much of a discount you can ask for from any given creditor.

This means you are likely to accept far less than you might have to. If they offer a 10–20 percent savings, you might rejoice, but this may still fall far short of what you could have saved through a professional intermediary.

Still, it might be worth a try, and it is definitely worth your effort with creditors that refuse to play ball with debt-resolution companies.

You might be wondering, "What happens to my FICO score if I do debt resolution?" It takes a hit because you are not "paying as agreed." This depleted score will probably last as long as your debts remain unpaid.

But remember this. If you are falling behind in your bills, your score has already taken a big hit, so the added disadvantage may be, relatively speaking, minimal.

Debt-resolution companies will tell you that FICO scores are good mainly for one thing: taking on more debt! Paying attention to your score is generally a wise idea, but it is really not your number-one priority if you want to get out of debt and back on an even keel financially.

Becoming emotionally detached from the meaning of your credit score is a necessary precursor to accessing the help of debt-resolution companies. They'll tell you that in most cases your bills must be at least ninety to 120 days delinquent, meaning unpaid, before creditors will speak to them and start to negotiate reductions.

This means you will be watching your credit score tank before debt settlers seem to be rolling up their sleeves. The only way you can permit this to occur with any equanimity is to reduce the importance of FICO score in your mind.

Seen in an inch-by-inch perspective, letting go of your emotional attachment to your FICO is an inch you have to give up in order to regain a yard of financial tranquility and balance.

Earlier in this section I mentioned bankruptcy. This may be a suitable recourse for you under certain conditions.

If your personal assets are few apart from the clothes on your back and some household items that can't fetch a substantial return at fire-sale prices, then you may want to consider it.

There are two kinds of personal bankruptcy: Chapter 7 and Chapter 11.

Chapter 7 is a complete discharging of your debts, though some are exempted from the proceedings and must be paid regardless. These include child and spousal support and some types of student loans. We'll talk about those student loans in a minute.

Chapter 11 requires creditors to be repaid at least a portion of what you owe them. The court authorizes a payment plan on the basis of your income and expenses.

You are permitted to retain certain assets without selling them. After all payments have been made, the bankruptcy is discharged.

The aim of bankruptcy is to provide people and companies with a means to find a fresh start, unencumbered by past debts. It is also a formal way to stop the incessant badgering of creditors. Once they have been notified that a bankruptcy petition has been filed, they are legally forbidden from contacting you directly.

Creditors can appear at a stated time in bankruptcy court to contest your petition or to ask for priority in a re-payment scheme. But they face penalties if they continue to contact you directly.

Bankruptcy is a drastic way to handle unpaid debt, but for many, it is necessary. You should seek advice from one or more bankruptcy lawyers before taking this step.

Once you have discharged your debts though bank-ruptcy, you are forbidden from filing another bankruptcy petition for eight years. Paradoxically, this makes you a decent credit risk to some lenders. You could be seeing direct-mail solicitations for credit cards in as few as six months after your bankruptcy is formally concluded.

Bear in mind that many of these offers will be at sky-high interest rates and will entitle you to access only meager credit lines. After a period of two or more years, lending terms will become more attractive.

One of the downsides of a bankruptcy is that it could appear on your credit report for a period of ten years. This could prevent you from accessing certain lenders who have an outright antipathy toward those that have resolved their debts in this manner.

There is another vital area in which consumers and businesspeople become ensnared: tax debt. This can be very distracting and of course expensive, with the penal-ties and interest that can accrue.

This is another area in which you can receive expert assistance. Tax-resolution firms exist that can negotiate with state and federal agencies to reduce your debts, but you need to qualify.

There are four basic forms of tax resolution: (1) offers in compromise; (2) tax-penalty abatements; (3) custom repayment plans; and (4) currently not collectible status.

The *offer in compromise* is what you may have heard blasting through your radio and popping up in ads on your Internet screens. It is by far the most inviting form of tax relief.

Essentially it involves tax forgiveness on the part of the authorities. You need to submit lists of your assets and liabilities and income and expenses. If you don't own real estate or other assets that have equity or cash value, then you might qualify for a reduction of your tax debts.

Proof of your current condition is required in the form of bills and receipts and prior tax returns. And as a condition of qualifying for most forms of tax resolution, your past tax returns must all be submitted or must be freshly prepared and then submitted.

Again, to repay merely pennies on the dollar may be too much to expect, despite what you've heard and seen in advertising. But you can garner substantial savings, providing you qualify.

Unlike debt-resolution companies, at this time tax-resolution firms may charge up-front fees. These can range into many thousands of dollars and are usually determined by the amount of tax debt you owe.

I should point out that one of the major complaints users have with regard to tax-resolution firms is that the latter charged a large fee and for the result they delivered, it was far too expensive.

If you owe $50,000, then you can expect to be quoted a fee of between $5000 and $10,000 to get it resolved. Will it be to your advantage in every case to use a tax-resolution firm?

Absolutely not. For one thing, they cannot guarantee what an agency of government will do in any given case. Private firms cannot compel outcomes. They can advise you about the likelihood of benefitting you in your case, but remember, they are biased in their own favor.

Not everyone, for instance, will qualify for an offer in compromise. Especially if you have assets that can be sold or borrowed against, the government will almost certainly put liens on them until you pay your tax debts down to their fullest extent.

At the same time, almost anyone could qualify for a customized payment plan. What you need to know is this: you can almost certainly formulate one with the government agency directly, at no extra cost to you.

You don't need a tax-resolution firm to make the call for you. You may wait on hold for a long time, but it is worth it to contact the IRS, for example, on your own.

Here is a crucial bit of negotiation advice for when you do: Tell them how much you feel you can afford to pay per month. If at that amount your tax debt cannot be retired within five years or less, it is likely that they'll refuse your offer. But they will probably tell you what they will accept, and this will be less than the monthly payment they'll ask for if you leave it up to them to make the first offer.

The key words are *payment plan*. You might begin the conversation by identifying yourself, and they'll ask you for some information and then the reason for your call.

You then say, "I wish I could pay this bill in full right now, but I'm going to need to work out a payment plan. I can pay up to $50 per month."

They could accept this if you own $3000 or less, or they might say, "We'll let you pay $50 this month and next, but starting in February, that will need to go up to $75."

This beats what they might have insisted on if you had asked, "How much do I need to pay per month?" and left it entirely up to them to decide.

I mentioned there is a *currently not collectible* (CNC) status. You could qualify for this if you are unemployed or disabled. Your debt doesn't go away. The taxing agency hopes that you'll recover your health and functions, or get a job, or even win the lottery.

CNC status is usually conferred for a year at a time and must be renewed. This means you could be asked to submit and to update certain income and expense statements annually.

Tax authorities sometimes agree to penalty and interest abatements to reduce and make more manageable your overall amount of debt. If you have never asked for or received this type of tax forgiveness, you might automatically qualify for a one-time savings, but you need to ask.

The good news is that there is a little-known statute of limitations that applies to the government's ability to collect old tax debts. Typically, after ten years, your debts to the IRS will no longer be pressed for payment by that agency.

State taxing authorities have their own statutes of limitation. You need to research what they are in your given case.

Also, some tax debts that are over three years old may be discharged in bankruptcy proceedings. You need to list all of your debts, including tax debts, and consult your legal counsel to determine if you qualify for tax relief through bankruptcy.

To review, these are some inch-by-inch approaches to restoring your financial balance. You should start by calling nonprofit agencies that can assist you with debt reduction and with tax resolution.

Contact for-profit firms to establish what they can do over and above what the nonprofits offer.

In extreme cases, you might consider bankruptcy, if only to catch your breath from debt collectors. You can choose Chapter 13, which will require submitting to a court-supervised and approved repayment plan.

Or you could seek a completely fresh start by discharging all qualifying debts. Don't be afraid to reach out to creditors and to taxing agencies to negotiate directly with them. In many cases, you'll be surprised at how much they do to assist clients to manage, reduce, and repay their obligations.

As you read or listen to this section, you should also know that approximately 48 million Americans are carrying student loan debt, which totals around $1.3

trillion. This is more than credit-card debt, if you can believe that.

Under the authority of the William D. Ford Act passed in 2007, you might qualify for a dramatically reduced payment based on your income. There are commercial companies that will charge you $500 and up to do the paperwork to consolidate your debts under the Ford Act, but this is something you can do for yourself.

After a certain number of months, usually 240, you can also have your remaining a student-loan debt balances cancelled. So it's possible to have a zero-dollar payment if your income is low, and then to have loan forgiveness at the end of a term.

If you work in public service or for a nonprofit, then your term could be curtailed to 120 months.

Contact studentloans.gov and NOT your loan-servicing company. The latter wants to keep you in debt, and only the government can permit you to smartly curtail your payments and qualify for debt forgiveness.

Take comfort in the fact that many others have gone through these financial trials before you, and many others are sure to follow. By taking an incremental approach to overcoming these problems, you could put yourself on the path to a far brighter future.

These woes won't stop you from achieving any goal. Remember: you can even become president of the United States!

Afterword

I hope you've enjoyed this material as much as I have enjoyed sharing it with you. Ever since I wrote and recorded my best-selling book *The Law of Large Numbers: How to Make Success Inevitable,* I felt we needed to make *Inch by Inch, It's a Cinch* as a complementary piece.

One program says, do a lot and you'll succeed. The other says, do *something*! Start! You just have to get under way in the most modest manner and you'll succeed.

Both messages are important, I think. As I've already said, by getting just one school to offer my seminar, I started something that I could multiply throughout the United States and then the world.

A tiny start followed by a massive follow-through is unimaginably powerful.

"Tell the tale and then go for scale." That's my motto, and I hope you'll make it yours.

Please look into my other books and audios, and stay tuned for more.

If you have any comments or questions, or if you'd like information about my speeches, seminars, classes, and coaching, please look me up. I can be reached at several email addresses, including gary@customersatisfaction.com, drgaryscottgoodman@yahoo.com, and gary@negotiationschool.com. And you can pick up the phone and reach me at (818) 970-GARY, which is (818) 970-4279.

In the meantime, all the best and great good luck to you!

Dr. Gary S. Goodman

Index

Printed in the USA
CPSIA information can be obtained
at www.ICGtesting.com
JSHW012028140824
68134JS00033B/2929